SOUPS

SIMPLE AND EASY
RECIPES FOR
SOUP-MAKING MACHINES

Norma Miller

RIGHT WAY

Constable & Robinson Ltd
55–56 Russell Square
London WC1B 4HP
www.constablerobinson.com

First published by Right Way,
an imprint of Constable & Robinson, 2012

A copy of the British Library Cataloguing in
Publication Data is available from the British Library

ISBN: 978-0-7160-2319-7

Typeset by TW Typesetting, Plymouth, Devon

Printed and bound in the EU

5 7 9 10 8 6

SOUPS

SIMPLE AND EASY RECIPES FOR SOUP-MAKING MACHINES

Other Cookery Titles in Right Way

The Halogen Oven Cookbook*
Waffles, Crêpes and Pancakes*
The Food Mixer Cookbook*
Slow Cooking Properly Explained
Slow Cooking: Best New Recipes
Steaming
Fresh Bread in the Morning from Your Bread Machine
Ice Cream Made Easy

Also by Norma Miller

CONTENTS

ACKNOWLEDGEMENTS

Thanks to the following for loan of equipment:

Cuisinart
www.cuisinart.co.uk
Customer Care 0870 240 6902

Waring
www.waringproducts.co.uk
Customer Care 0870 060 4260

INTRODUCTION

Soups to savour, soups to stimulate, soups to satisfy, soups in endless variety. With your own soup maker the world of soup opens up like you've never known it before. All kinds of textures and flavours, lots of healthy and tasty ingredients, and always the possibility of something new, something different, something exciting.

There are two types of appliance, a blender-style soup maker and a jug-style soup maker. These are both described in the following pages, and the recipes are suitable and adapted for both types of machine. Whichever type of soup maker you use, all the recipes in this book should be easy and fun to make. Simplicity is the watchword, and cooking skills and experience can be at a minimum.

There are traditional favourites, such as mulligatawny soup, creamy tomato and basil soup, pea and ham soup and corn chowder; there are contemporary and innovative recipes, including prawn and saffron soup with noodles, Thai chicken and red chilli soup, and chilled cherry and almond soup; and then there are hints and tips for improvising on the recipes with your own favourite flavour combinations.

There is something immensely enjoyable about sitting down to a bowl of delicious, home-made soup, with its intense or subtle flavours perfectly matched to your mood and situation. To bring this pleasure about so much more easily, maintain a good stock of spices and store-cupboard essentials, be sure to have top-quality fresh ingredients to hand, and always keep your soup maker at the ready.

Before you start
- The whole process of cooking in a soup maker can be speedier than when making soup conventionally in a pan on the hob. Before you

begin to cook, it's a good idea to gather together and prepare all the ingredients you will need.

- For best results cut ingredients into thin slices or 2.5 cm/1 inch dice.
- Never overfill the soup maker; the maximum capacity for the total volume of ingredients is marked on the machine and is to be found in the instruction booklet which comes with the appliance.
- The recipes are a guide; machines vary, and vegetables and fruits are never standard in shape and size.
- Throughout the book I've referred to the blender-style soup maker as having a glass jar in which the ingredients are put, and the jug-style soup maker as having a metal jug in which the ingredients are put.
- When in use, the surfaces of the machine will become very hot.
- To prevent damage to the motor it is important to use the blend function continuously only for the time mentioned in the handbook for your particular machine. It may be as little as one minute for one particular model or three minutes for another. Allow the machine to cool before using the blend function again.
- The recipes take into account the two types of machines with the method instructions for the blender-style soup maker first and the method for the jug-style soup maker at the end of the recipe.
- Soup is only as good as the quality of the ingredients, especially the stock. Use the best quality available that is full of flavour.

The soup maker – what is it?
It is a portable, free-standing electric appliance which cooks and blends ingredients to make a soup the consistency of your choice, chunky or smooth. Conveniently, it just needs to be plugged into an earthed mains power socket.

There are two types of machines available on the market – a blender-style soup maker and a jug-style soup maker. Each type of machine works slightly differently.

Blender-style soup maker
This type of soup maker looks rather like a conventional blender, but is heavier. These machines are more expensive, but they do have extra features and functions which give great flexibility. With no pre-programmed settings to cook and blend the raw ingredients you are in control of the whole process, whether browning onions, deciding how long you simmer the soup for, or adding extra ingredients part way through. Even noodles can be added later in the process to heat through because they won't be blended to a pulp.

This soup maker consists of a glass jar section which is a complete unit: the glass jar; a handle, a non-stick cooking plate and a collar with blades. The assembly sits on the powerful motor base. The lid has a removable measuring cup which must be in place when the soup is

Fig. 1. Blender-style soup maker

cooking and blending. Simple to use controls are on the base motor unit. An on/off power button puts the machine in stand-by mode. The blending control dial lets you choose between four settings from low to high speed as well as a pulse setting, so there is plenty of control over how chunky or smooth the soup can be. For safety, the blending control only works when the cooking or heating process has completed. *To prevent damage to the motor it is important to use the blend function continuously only for the time mentioned in the handbook for your particular machine. It may be as little as one minute for one particular model or three minutes for another. Allow the machine to cool before using the blend function again.* The stir button is useful as it can be used at any time, whilst onions are frying or just to mix the ingredients together when they all go into the glass jar. The timer control can be adjusted from one to thirty minutes. Heat or temperature controls will start the cooking cycle. Select from either high, low or simmer. The temperature can be changed at any time during the heating or cooking cycle.

This machine can be used as a traditional blender to mix cold ingredients and to crush ice. A great function of this machine, especially for soup making, is that ingredients such as onions and garlic can be browned, fried or sautéed in a little oil and butter (poured or dropped onto the cooking plate rather than the blades) in the base of the machine adding great flavour. The glass jar lets you see the food cooking, which is an advantage. It is normal for steam to escape around the measuring cup, so handle with care. Soups bubble up during cooking, so the maximum fill level for blending hot ingredients is less than for blending cold ingredients, and both are marked on the side of the glass jar.

Extra ingredients which need little cooking can be added part-way through the cooking process; either stop the machine, or reduce the temperature to simmer. Using oven gloves, carefully remove the measuring cup and wait until the built-up steam disperses (to avoid scalding). Carefully add the ingredients and replace the measuring cup. Start the machine and continue cooking.

Let the machine cool before making a second batch of soup.

Raw meat or fish and frozen vegetables can be used in this type of soup maker.

Jug-style soup maker

This type of soup maker looks rather like a large metal lidded jug, but is heavier. The lid is the motor unit with built-in blender blades and an overfill sensor. A plastic measuring jug is a useful extra. Soups bubble up during cooking, so the maximum fill level is marked on the side of the metal jug. There is also a minimum level because the blades have to reach the ingredients. The jug is metal not glass so it's essential to check the levels each time you cook.

Fig. 2. Jug-style soup maker

Very, very simple and easy to use as it has two automatic pre-programmed soup settings to cook and blend ingredients. There are just three function buttons to operate the machine, marked purée, chunky and blend/clean.

Option 1 – Put the ingredients into the metal jug and fit the lid in place. Press the purée button and the soup maker is automatically programmed to heat and blend the soup. This takes about 20–25 minutes.

Option 2 – Put the ingredients into the metal jug and fit the lid in place. Select and press the chunky button and the soup maker is automatically programmed to heat the soup (this option is not programmed to automatically blend the soup). This takes about 30 minutes. At this stage you can carefully lift the lid and add any final ingredients such as chopped fresh herbs or cream. Replace the lid and press the blend/clean button, if necessary, to alter the consistency.

This style of machine does not have a function for browning onions.

For safety the blending control only works when the cooking or heating process has completed. *To prevent damage to the motor it is important to use the blend function continuously only for the time mentioned in the handbook for your particular machine. It may be as little as one minute for one particular model or three minutes for another. Allow the machine to cool before using the blend function again.*

- Don't use the machine when empty.
- Let the machine cool before making a second batch of soup.
- Some food **cannot** be used in this type of soup maker. Do **not** use raw meat or fish/shellfish. Do **not** use cooked meat or fish which has been frozen. Only use cooked meat, cooked fish or cooked shelled seafood. Let frozen vegetables and fruits thaw before use.

Note: For both types of machine

- For obvious reasons you cannot make soups using shellfish in their shells or meat with any bones in either type of machine.
- Both machines are quite heavy when full of piping hot soup. You may prefer to ladle the soup into bowls rather than pour from the glass jar or metal jug.

Care and cleaning

- Read the 'important safety advice section' (see opposite).
- Unplug the machine before cleaning.
- Allow the soup maker to cool before cleaning.
- If the machine has a 'self-cleaning' feature, follow the manufacturer's instructions.
- Do not clean the machine or accessories in a dishwasher.
- Avoid cleaning the soup maker with any abrasive cleaners or scouring pads.

- If necessary, use a pan brush to clean any stubborn stains.
- Take care not to touch the blades as they are very sharp.
- Depending on the type of machine, the inside of the glass jar or metal jug can be cleaned with hot soapy water.
- Wipe the outside of the soup maker with a damp cloth to clean.

Important safety advice

Much of this advice should be common sense when using any kitchen appliance:

- The soup maker must be on a stable heat-proof surface and not near the edge of work surfaces.
- Keep the surrounding areas clear and free from clutter.
- Ensure there is adequate air space around the soup maker for air to circulate.
- Only use the soup maker indoors.
- Don't move the machine when in use.
- Don't leave the soup maker unattended whilst in use.
- Make sure the power cord is not touching anything hot.
- Don't use the appliance when empty.
- Don't put your hands on the blades.
- Before starting to cook in the soup maker, make sure the lid is securely on top of the machine.
- Keep children and pets away from the soup maker when in use.
- Don't immerse the machine, power cord or electric plug in hot water or place in a dishwasher.
- Don't put the machine away until it is cold.
- If any faults occur with your soup maker, always contact the manufacturer.

Adapting your own recipes for the soup maker

You probably have several favourite soup recipes that you'd usually cook on the hob or in a microwave oven. Many of these may be suitable to adapt to make in the soup maker. You just need to experiment a little. Bear in mind the manufacturer's guidelines for using your particular soup maker, such as whether or not ingredients can go into the machine raw or frozen. Often it's just a matter of letting the frozen vegetables or fruits thaw and using cooked meats in place of raw. Your soup maker has a maximum capacity for the total volume of all the liquids and the prepared ingredients. As a rough guide, I add up all the liquid weights, the stock, water, tomato juice, cream or yogurt in the recipe. If this is around 700 ml/1¼ pints then with other chopped ingredients it should fit into your soup maker. If the quantities are too large for your machine, reduce by a quarter, a third or a half. When reducing quantities, remember to reduce the spices and herbs as well. (It's a matter of being aware of what your machine is capable of, and then trying things out and experimenting.)

Tips for using the soup maker

- Never leave the machine unattended when it is in use.
- Cut most foods into small dice to ensure they cook evenly.
- I like to use granular stock or stock cubes dissolved in boiling water from the kettle. This will help the cooking process.
- As soup makers are sealed units during the cooking process, the liquid doesn't evaporate and doesn't therefore concentrate the flavours as happens in a saucepan on the hob – so do taste for seasoning before serving.
- The blender-style machines have a useful measuring cup in the lid. After use, always replace in the lid as the hot liquid could splash out of the machine.
- For machines with a browning or frying function, pour a little oil or butter onto the blades before adding the onions to soften – this will prevent them sticking.
- If the soup is too thick, thin the soup with a little boiling water poured from the kettle.
- Ready-cooked rice, noodles, pasta and pulses can be heated in a microwave oven until piping hot to be stirred immediately into bowls of soup.

About the recipes

- The recipes are a guide. Machines vary, and vegetables and fruits are never standard in shape and size.
- The recipes take into account the differences between the two types of machine with the method instructions for the blender-style soup maker first and the method for the jug-style soup maker at the end of the recipe.
- All the recipes have been designed for cooking in a soup maker, and the preparation and cooking processes for each recipe are straightforward and easy to follow.
- In many of the recipes I've used the vegetables and other ingredients to thicken the soups. If after trying a recipe you would prefer a thicker soup the next time you make it, just add a little flour or cornflour.
- Throughout the book there are plenty of serving suggestions and hints and tips to go with the recipes.
- Mostly the recipes make two to four servings, depending on whether they are eaten as a snack, a starter or a main meal.
- For convenience, the recipe ingredients are listed in the order in which they are used. Though they are given in imperial as well as metric, you will find the metric measurements easier.
- All spoon measures are level unless otherwise stated.

- The recipes are often adaptable, and you can easily substitute interchangeable ingredients (your choice) as long as they don't exceed the capacity of the machine.
- For these recipes I have used a mixture of fresh seasonal produce, store-cupboard ingredients, canned foods, as well as some frozen items.
- For speedy soups I often make use of sachets of pre-cooked varieties of rice, pulses, pasta and noodles.
- My store-cupboard always contains a wide selection of spices and spice mixes, and small jars of pastes and purées that are so quick and convenient.
- Salt is included in some of the recipes, but use with discretion.
- If you are preparing food for someone who has a food allergy, be sure to study the list of ingredients carefully.
- Some recipes contain fresh chillies. Do take care when preparing them and remember to wash your hands thoroughly afterwards. Better still, wear rubber gloves while handling them.
- Remember to taste and season the soups if necessary before serving.

1

CHILLED SOUPS

If it's a hot day and you're hungry, if you're in need of something light, tasty and refreshing, if you want a dish to spark you up and cool you down, then this is where to look. Bright and colourful to behold, these chilled soup recipes are perfect for summertime – so cool, so smooth and so invigorating, with their aromatic, spicy and peppery flavours.

Chilled soups can be made by processing raw ingredients, but I like to cook the ingredients for these soups and then chill. Smaller portions are usual for chilled soups, so these recipes serve 4–6 people. Have crushed ice cubes available to stir in at the table.

Of course, chilled soups can be delicious at any time of the year.

Chilled Spiced Melon and Cucumber Soup

Very refreshing, even though there's some 'heat' from the spices.

Serves 4–6

1 shallot
5 cm/2 inch piece of fresh root ginger
1 melon, to give about 500 g/1 lb 2 oz flesh
1 cucumber
1 red chilli (see page 17)
Bunch of fresh coriander
1 tbsp sunflower oil
½ tsp mild curry powder
600 ml/1 pint vegetable stock
150 ml/¼ pint natural yogurt
Salt and freshly milled black pepper, to taste

Coriander leaves, to serve

1. Finely chop the shallot. Coarsely grate the root ginger, gather together with your hand and squeeze the juice into a cup. Discard the pulp. Peel the melon, cut in half and scoop out the seeds. Cut the flesh into small cubes, about 2.5 cm/1 inch. Cut the cucumber in half lengthways, scoop out the seeds and thinly slice. Cut the chilli in half, remove and discard the seeds and finely chop. Remove the coriander leaves from the stalks.
2. *Blender-style soup maker* – Put the oil into the glass jar. Set the timer to 20 minutes and the temperature to low. Add the chopped shallot, cover and cook for 1–2 minutes using the stir button occasionally until just lightly browned and starting to soften.
3. Remove the lid and add the remaining ingredients except the yogurt. Cover, stir to mix and raise the temperature to high. Bring to the boil, then reduce the heat to simmer and cook for the remaining time using the stir button occasionally. Pour in the yogurt, cover and blend until smooth.
4. If necessary, season to taste. Ladle or pour the soup into a large bowl, leave to cool and chill until required. Serve in bowls with a few coriander leaves scattered over.

Jug-style soup maker
Put all the prepared ingredients (step 1 above) and other ingredients, except the yogurt, into the metal jug. (The level of total ingredients must be above the minimum mark and below the maximum.) Secure the lid in place. Select the purée function and leave to cook. Stir in the yogurt and season to taste, if necessary. See step 4 above for chilling and serving the soup.

Chilled Tomato and Olive Soup

Rather like gazpacho, but here the ingredients are cooked first and then chilled.

Serves 4–6

1 large red onion	1 tbsp red wine vinegar
3 garlic cloves	½ tsp sugar
2 medium red peppers	400 g can tomatoes
2 medium courgettes	150 ml/¼ pint passata
Small bunch of basil	600 ml/1 pint vegetable stock
Several small stoned black olives	Salt and freshly milled black pepper,
2 tbsp olive oil	to taste

Basil leaves, olive oil, crushed ice cubes, crusty bread, to serve

1. Finely chop the onion and crush the garlic. Cut the red peppers in half, remove the stalks and seeds and thinly slice. Dice the courgettes and pull the leaves from the basil. Thinly slice the black olives and put in a small bowl.
2. *Blender-style soup maker* – Put the oil into the glass jar. Set the timer to 30 minutes and the temperature to high. Add the onion and garlic, cover and cook for 1 minute using the stir button occasionally. Add the red pepper and courgettes, cover and cook for 1–2 minutes until steaming using the stir button occasionally.
3. Remove the lid and add the remaining ingredients except the sliced black olives. Cover, stir to mix and bring to the boil, then reduce the heat to simmer and cook for the remaining time using the stir button occasionally. Blend to the consistency you prefer. Add the olives and stir.
4. If necessary, season to taste. Ladle or pour the soup into a large bowl, leave to cool and chill until required. Serve in bowls with a few basil leaves scattered over and a few drops of olive oil drizzled over. Spoon a little crushed ice in the centre.

Jug-style soup maker
Put all the prepared ingredients (step 1 above) and other ingredients, except the sliced olives, into the metal jug. (The level of total ingredients must be above the minimum mark and below the maximum.) Secure the lid in place. Select the purée function and leave to cook. Stir in the sliced olives and season to taste, if necessary. See step 4 above for chilling and serving the soup.

Chilled Vichyssoise

A different take on the classic leek and potato soup.

Serves 4–6

1 large onion
2 garlic cloves
1 large leek
1 large potato
2 tbsp olive oil
Small handful of parsley sprigs
150 ml/¼ pint milk
600 ml/1 pint vegetable or chicken stock
150 ml/¼ pint single cream
Salt and freshly milled white pepper, to taste

Chopped chives and torn focaccia bread, to serve

1. Finely chop the onion and crush the garlic. Thinly slice the leek. Finely chop the potato.
2. *Blender-style soup maker* – Put the oil into the glass jar. Set the timer to 30 minutes and the temperature to high. Add the onion and garlic, cover and cook for 1 minute using the stir button occasionally. Add the sliced leek, cover and cook for 1–2 minutes until steaming using the stir button occasionally.
3. Remove the lid and add the remaining ingredients except the cream. Cover, stir to mix and bring to the boil for 2–3 minutes, then reduce the heat to simmer and cook for the remaining time using the stir button occasionally. Blend to the consistency you prefer. Pour in the cream, cover and stir for a second or two.
4. If necessary, season to taste. Ladle or pour the soup into a large bowl, leave to cool and chill until required. Serve in bowls with a sprinkling of chopped chives on top and torn pieces of focaccia bread on the side.

Jug-style soup maker
Put all the prepared ingredients (step 1 above) and other ingredients, except the cream, into the metal jug. (The level of total ingredients must be above the minimum mark and below the maximum.) Secure the lid in place. Select the chunky function and leave to cook. Blend to the consistency you prefer. Stir in the cream and season to taste, if necessary. See step 4 above for chilling and serving the soup.

Chilled Rocket and Watercress Soup

Simple ingredients, but so much flavour from spicy tangy rocket and peppery watercress.

Serves 4–6

1 large onion
1 large potato
2 bunches of watercress
2 tbsp olive oil
2 large handfuls of rocket leaves
600 ml/1 pint milk
4–6 tbsp unsweetened orange juice
700 ml/1 pint vegetable or chicken stock
150 ml/¼ pint single cream
Salt and freshly milled black pepper, to taste

Wedges of orange, to serve

1. Finely chop the onion and cut the potato into small cubes. Discard any tough watercress stalks and roughly chop.
2. *Blender-style soup maker* – Put the oil into the glass jar. Set the timer to 30 minutes and the temperature to high. Add the onion, cover and cook for 1 minute using the stir button occasionally. Remove the lid and add the remaining ingredients except the cream. Cover, stir to mix and bring to the boil for 2–3 minutes, then reduce the heat to simmer and cook for the remaining time using the stir button occasionally. Blend to the consistency you prefer. Pour in the cream, cover and stir for a second or two.
3. If necessary, season to taste. Ladle or pour the soup into a large bowl, leave to cool and chill until required. Serve in bowls with a wedge of orange, to squeeze over.

Jug-style soup maker
Put all the prepared ingredients (step 1 above) and other ingredients, except the cream, into the metal jug. (The level of total ingredients must be above the minimum mark and below the maximum.) Secure the lid in place. Select the chunky function and leave to cook. Blend to the consistency you prefer. Stir in the cream and season to taste, if necessary. See step 3 above for chilling and serving the soup.

Chilled Beetroot Soup

A flavourful soup with an amazing colour.

Serves 4–6

1 large red onion
1 small potato
4 cooked beetroot
1 orange
Small bunch of fennel leaves
2 tbsp sunflower oil
850 ml/1 ½ pints chicken or vegetable stock
Salt and freshly milled black pepper, to taste

Soured cream or crème fraîche and a few tiny fennel leaves, to serve

1. Finely chop the onion and cut the potato and beetroot into small cubes. Finely grate the rind from half of the orange, cut in half and squeeze the juice from both halves. Roughly chop the fennel leaves.
2. *Blender-style soup maker* – Put the oil into the glass jar. Set the timer to 30 minutes and the temperature to high. Add the onion, cover and cook for 1 minute using the stir button occasionally. Remove the lid and add the remaining ingredients. Cover, stir to mix and bring to the boil for 2–3 minutes, then reduce the heat to simmer and cook for the remaining time using the stir button occasionally. Blend to the consistency you prefer.
3. If necessary, season to taste. Ladle or pour the soup into a large bowl, leave to cool and chill until required. Serve in bowls topped with a swirl of soured cream or crème fraîche and scatter over a few fennel leaves.

Jug-style soup maker
Put all the prepared ingredients (step 1 above) and other ingredients into the metal jug. (The level of total ingredients must be above the minimum mark and below the maximum.) Secure the lid in place. Select the chunky function and leave to cook. Blend to the consistency you prefer. Season to taste, if necessary. See step 3 above for chilling and serving the soup.

Chilled Green Pea and Broad Bean Soup

Chilled soups are very refreshing on hot summer days. If fresh mint is unavailable just add a dash of mint sauce.

Serves 4–6

6 spring onions
1 small potato
4 sprigs of mint
2 tbsp olive oil
250 g/9 oz peas, fresh or frozen
250 g/9 oz broad beans, fresh or frozen
700 ml/1 ¼ pints chicken or vegetable stock
Salt and freshly milled black pepper, to taste

Yogurt and hot crusty bread, to serve

1. Thinly slice the spring onions. Cut the potato into small pieces. Pull the mint leaves from the stalks.
2. *Blender-style soup maker* – Put the oil into the glass jar. Set the timer to 30 minutes and the temperature to high. Add the onion, cover and cook for 1 minute using the stir button occasionally. Remove the lid and add the remaining ingredients. Cover, stir to mix and bring to the boil for 2–3 minutes, then reduce the heat to simmer and cook for the remaining time using the stir button occasionally. Blend to the consistency you prefer.
3. If necessary, season to taste. Ladle or pour the soup into a large bowl, leave to cool and chill until required. Serve in bowls topped with a spoonful of yogurt and hot crusty bread on the side.

Jug-style soup maker
Thaw the peas and broad beans, if frozen.

Put all the prepared ingredients (step 1 above) and other ingredients into the metal jug. (The level of total ingredients must be above the minimum mark and below the maximum.) Secure the lid in place. Select the chunky function and leave to cook. Blend to the consistency you prefer. Season to taste, if necessary. See step 3 above for chilling and serving the soup.

Chilled Radish, Pepper and Lettuce Soup

One of my favourite soups. For such a thin soup, there's a surprising sensation of heat and pepper. Serve with a glass of vodka or gin and warm breadsticks.

Serves 4–6

2 bunches of radishes
6–8 spring onions
1 red pepper
½ small lettuce
1 lime
1 tbsp olive oil
850 ml/1 ½ pints chicken or vegetable stock
Salt and freshly milled black pepper, to taste

Lime slice, to serve

1. Thinly slice the radishes and spring onions. Cut the red pepper in half, remove the stalk and seeds and thinly slice. Pull the leaves from the lettuce stalk and chop or tear into small pieces. Grate the rind from the lime (you will need about 1 tsp), cut in half and squeeze out the juice.
2. *Blender-style soup maker* – Put the oil into the glass jar. Set the timer to 20 minutes and the temperature to low. Add the spring onions, cover and cook for 2 minutes using the stir button occasionally until they begin to steam, but without browning too much.
3. Remove the lid and add the remaining ingredients. Cover, stir to mix, and bring just to the boil. Reduce the heat to simmer and cook for the remaining time using the stir button occasionally. Blend to the consistency you prefer.
4. If necessary, season to taste. Ladle or pour the soup into a large bowl, leave to cool and chill until required. Serve in bowls topped with a slice of lime.

Jug-style soup maker
Put all the prepared ingredients (step 1 above) and other ingredients into the metal jug. (The level of total ingredients must be above the minimum mark and below the maximum.) Secure the lid in place. Select the chunky function and leave to cook. Blend to the consistency you prefer. Season to taste, if necessary. See step 4 above for chilling and serving the soup.

Chilled Green Soup with Lemongrass

Lemongrass gives a sour-lemon taste to a dish. It can be very woody, so look out for a fresh tender piece.

Serves 4–6

6 spring onions
2 medium potatoes
1 green pepper
1 stick of fresh lemongrass
1 bunch of watercress
Small bunch of parsley
2 tbsp olive oil
3 large handfuls of small mixed salad leaves, such as rocket, beet, spinach
850 ml/1 ½ pints vegetable or chicken stock
Salt and freshly milled black pepper, to taste

Small leaves, to serve

1. Thinly slice the spring onions and cut the potatoes into small cubes. Cut the pepper in half, remove the stalk and seeds and thinly slice. Pull the tough outer leaves from the lemongrass and finely chop. Discard any tough watercress stalks and roughly chop with the parsley.
2. *Blender-style soup maker* – Put the oil into the glass jar. Set the timer to 25 minutes and the temperature to high. Add the spring onions, cover and cook for 1 minute using the stir button occasionally. Remove the lid and add the remaining ingredients. Cover, stir to mix and bring to the boil for 2–3 minutes, then reduce the heat to simmer and cook for the remaining time using the stir button occasionally. Blend to the consistency you prefer.
3. If necessary, season to taste. Ladle or pour the soup into a large bowl, leave to cool and chill until required. Serve in bowls with a few leaves scattered over.

Jug-style soup maker
Put all the prepared ingredients (step 1 above) and other ingredients into the metal jug. (The level of total ingredients must be above the minimum mark and below the maximum.) Secure the lid in place. Select the chunky function and leave to cook. Blend to the consistency you prefer. Season to taste, if necessary. See step 3 above for chilling and serving the soup.

2

SOUP MEDLEY

A dazzling variety of delicious hot soups is on offer in this and the next four chapters. There are lots of traditional-style soup recipes, with variations and some surprises as well. This is warming, comforting food, using familiar and widely-available ingredients – some meat and fish soups, and always an interesting mix of vegetables, herbs and spices.

Spring Vegetable Soup

Young, tiny, early-season vegetables give a lovely fresh taste to this colourful dish.

Serves 2–4

2 shallots
500 g/1 lb 2 oz selection of mini vegetables, such as carrots, courgettes, turnips, leeks
3 large handfuls of small spinach leaves
2 tbsp sunflower oil
1 tbsp wholegrain mustard
3 tbsp chopped parsley
Large pinch of grated nutmeg
700 ml/1 ¼ pints vegetable or chicken stock
Salt and freshly milled black pepper, to taste

Pecorino or Parmesan shavings, to serve

1. Finely chop the shallots. Cut the selection of mini vegetables into small pieces, either dice or slice. Tear the spinach leaves in half, if large.
2. *Blender-style soup maker* – Put the oil into the glass jar. Set the timer to 25 minutes and the temperature to high. Add the shallots, cover and cook for 1–2 minutes using the stir button occasionally until they begin to steam, but without browning too much.
3. Remove the lid and add the remaining ingredients. Cover, stir to mix and bring to the boil. Reduce the heat to simmer and cook for the remaining time using the stir button occasionally. Leave the soup chunky or blend to the consistency you prefer.
4. If necessary, season to taste. Ladle or pour the piping hot soup into bowls. Scatter over a few Pecorino or Parmesan shavings and serve immediately.

Jug-style soup maker
Put all the prepared ingredients (step 1 above) and other ingredients into the metal jug. (The level of total ingredients must be above the minimum mark and below the maximum.) Secure the lid in place. Select the chunky function and leave to cook. Season to taste, if necessary, and blend to the consistency you prefer. Serve as in step 4 above.

Celeriac and Red Onion Soup

Celeriac is a knobbly root vegetable tasting like a cross between celery and parsley.

Serves 2–4

3 red onions
1 celeriac, about 500 g/1 lb 2 oz
2 celery sticks
1 tbsp olive oil
2 tbsp lemon juice
700 ml/1 ¼ pints chicken or vegetable stock
Salt and freshly milled black pepper, to taste

Toasted breadcrumbs, to serve

1. Finely chop the onions. Peel the celeriac and cut into small cubes. Thinly slice the celery.
2. *Blender-style soup maker* – Put the oil into the glass jar. Set the timer to 30 minutes and the temperature to high. Add the onions, cover and cook for 2 minutes using the stir button occasionally until they begin to steam, but without browning too much. Add the celeriac and celery, cover, stir and cook for 5 minutes, using the stir button occasionally, until they begin to steam.
3. Add the remaining ingredients. Cover, stir to mix and bring to the boil for 2–3 minutes. Reduce the heat to simmer and cook for the remaining time using the stir button occasionally. Blend to the consistency you prefer. If necessary, season to taste.
4. Ladle or pour the piping hot soup into bowls. Scatter a few toasted breadcrumbs on top and serve immediately.

Jug-style soup maker
Put all the prepared ingredients (step 1 above) and other ingredients into the metal jug. (The level of total ingredients must be above the minimum mark and below the maximum.) Secure the lid in place. Select the purée function and leave to cook. Season to taste, if necessary, and serve the soup as in step 4 above.

Potato, Cheese and Herb Soup

No need to heat the cheese, it will melt with the heat of the soup.

Serves 2–4

1 large onion
2 garlic cloves
1 medium potato
1 tbsp olive oil
25 g/1 oz butter
¼ tsp freshly grated nutmeg
300 ml/½ pint milk
300 ml/½ pint chicken or vegetable stock
4 tbsp yogurt or crème fraîche
3 tbsp chopped mixed herbs – parsley, chives, chervil
4 tbsp grated mature Cheddar cheese
Salt and freshly milled white pepper, to taste

Grated cheese and breadsticks (page 123), to serve

1. Finely chop the onion and crush the garlic. Chop the potato into small pieces.
2. *Blender-style soup maker* – Put the oil and butter into the glass jar. Set the timer to 30 minutes and the temperature to high. Add the onion and garlic, cover and cook for 1 minute using the stir button occasionally. Add the potato, cover and cook for 1–2 minutes until steaming using the stir button occasionally.
3. Remove the lid and add the remaining ingredients except the yogurt or crème fraîche, herbs and cheese. Cover, stir to mix and bring to the boil for 2–3 minutes, then reduce the heat to simmer and cook for the remaining time, using the stir button occasionally. Blend to the consistency you prefer. Pour in the yogurt or crème fraîche, herbs and cheese, cover and stir for a second or two.
4. If necessary, season to taste. Ladle or pour the piping hot soup into bowls. Serve topped with a little grated cheese and breadsticks on the side. Serve immediately.

Jug-style soup maker
Put all the prepared ingredients (step 1 above) and other ingredients, except the yogurt or crème fraîche, herbs and cheese, into the metal jug. (The level of total ingredients must be above the minimum mark and below the maximum.) Secure the lid in place. Select the chunky function and leave to cook. Blend to the consistency you prefer, stir in the yogurt or crème fraîche, herbs and cheese, and season to taste if necessary. Serve the soup as in step 4 above.

Red Lentil Soup

These lentils do not need soaking before going into the soup maker.

Serves 2–4

1 medium red onion
1 celery stick
2 medium carrots
1 red chilli (see page 17)
1 tbsp olive oil
½ tsp dried mixed herbs
1½ tsp ground coriander
1½ tsp ground cumin
400 g can tomatoes
150 ml/¼ pint passata
600 ml/1 pint vegetable or chicken stock
140 g/5 oz red split lentils
Salt and freshly milled black pepper, to taste

Small celery leaves, to serve

1. Finely chop the onion. Thinly slice the celery and roughly chop the carrots into small cubes. Cut the chilli in half, remove the stalk and seeds and thinly slice.
2. *Blender-style soup maker* – Put the oil into the glass jar. Set the timer to 30 minutes and the temperature to high. Add the onion, cover and cook for 1–2 minutes using the stir button occasionally until it begins to steam, but without browning too much. Add the celery and carrot, cover, stir and cook for 5 minutes, using the stir button occasionally, until they begin to steam.
3. Add the remaining ingredients. Cover, stir to mix and bring to the boil for 2 minutes. Reduce the heat to simmer and cook for the remaining time using the stir button occasionally. Blend to the consistency you prefer. If necessary, season to taste.
4. Ladle or pour the piping hot soup into bowls. Top with celery leaves and serve immediately.

Jug-style soup maker
Put all the prepared ingredients (step 1 above) and other ingredients into the metal jug. (The level of total ingredients must be above the minimum mark and below the maximum.) Secure the lid in place. Select the purée function and leave to cook. Season to taste, if necessary, and serve the soup as in step 4 above.

Squash and Tomato Soup

A lovely combination of flavours and colours.

Serves 2–4

1 onion
400 g/14 oz wedge of butternut squash
1 medium potato
6 tomatoes
2 tbsp vegetable oil
Handful of basil leaves
2 tbsp tomato purée
Pinch of sugar
700 ml/1 ¼ pints vegetable or chicken stock
Salt and freshly milled black pepper, to taste

Olive oil to drizzle and a few basil leaves, to serve

1. Finely chop the onion. Remove any seeds from the butternut squash, peel and cut into small cubes with the potato. Chop the tomatoes.
2. *Blender-style soup maker* – Put the oil into the glass jar. Set the timer to 30 minutes and the temperature to high. Add the onion, cover and cook for 1–2 minutes using the stir button occasionally until it begins to steam, but without browning too much.
3. Remove the lid and add the remaining ingredients. Cover, stir to mix and bring to the boil. Reduce the heat to simmer and cook for the remaining time using the stir button occasionally. Blend to the consistency you prefer. If necessary, season to taste.
4. Ladle or pour the piping hot soup into bowls. Drizzle a little oil on top and scatter over the basil leaves. Serve immediately.

Jug-style soup maker
Put all the prepared ingredients (step 1 above) and other ingredients into the metal jug. (The level of total ingredients must be above the minimum mark and below the maximum.) Secure the lid in place. Select the purée function and leave to cook. Season to taste, if necessary, and serve the soup as in step 4 above.

Courgette, Green Pepper and Tarragon Soup

Tarragon provides an unmistakable anise flavour.

Serves 2–4

1 onion
2 green peppers
2 courgettes
2 medium potatoes
Large bunch of tarragon
1 tbsp sunflower oil
850 ml/1 ½ pints vegetable or chicken stock
Salt and freshly milled black pepper, to taste

Tarragon leaves, to serve

1. Finely chop the onion. Cut the peppers in half, remove the stalk and seeds and thinly slice. Chop the courgettes and potatoes into small pieces. Pull the tarragon leaves from the stalks and roughly chop.
2. *Blender-style soup maker* – Put the oil into the glass jar. Set the timer to 25 minutes and the temperature to high. Add the onion, cover and cook for 1–2 minutes using the stir button occasionally until beginning to steam, but without browning too much. Add the peppers and courgettes, cover and cook for 5 minutes using the stir button occasionally until beginning to steam.
3. Remove the lid and add the remaining ingredients. Cover, stir to mix and bring to the boil. Reduce the heat to simmer and cook for the remaining time using the stir button occasionally. Leave the soup chunky or blend to the consistency you prefer.
4. If necessary, season to taste. Ladle or pour the piping hot soup into bowls. Scatter over a few tarragon leaves and serve immediately.

Jug-style soup maker

Put all the prepared ingredients (step 1 above) and other ingredients into the metal jug. (The level of total ingredients must be above the minimum mark and below the maximum.) Secure the lid in place. Select the chunky function and leave to cook. Season to taste, if necessary, and blend to the consistency you prefer. Serve as in step 4 above.

Sweetcorn and Pepper Soup

Pungent and slightly bitter, the sage is a perfect foil for the sweetcorn.

Serves 2–4

1 onion
2 celery sticks
2 peppers, yellow and orange
280 g/10 oz sweetcorn kernels, fresh, canned or frozen
4 sage leaves
1 tbsp olive oil
700 ml/1 ¼ pints vegetable or chicken stock
Salt and freshly milled black pepper, to taste

Celery leaves, to serve

1. Finely chop the onion. Thinly slice the celery sticks. Cut the peppers in half, remove the stalks and seeds and thinly slice. Drain the sweetcorn – if using canned. Finely chop the sage leaves.
2. *Blender-style soup maker* – Put the oil into the glass jar. Set the timer to 25 minutes and the temperature to high. Add the onion, cover and cook for 1–2 minutes using the stir button occasionally until beginning to brown a little. Add the celery and yellow and orange peppers, cover and cook for 5–6 minutes using the stir button occasionally until beginning to steam.
3. Remove the lid and add the remaining ingredients. Cover, stir to mix and bring to the boil for 2 minutes. Reduce the heat to simmer and cook for the remaining time using the stir button occasionally. Blend until still chunky.
4. If necessary, season to taste. Ladle or pour the piping hot soup into bowls. Top with a celery leaf and serve immediately.

Jug-style soup maker
Thaw frozen sweetcorn.

Put all the prepared ingredients (step 1 above) and other ingredients into the metal jug. (The level of total ingredients must be above the minimum mark and below the maximum.) Secure the lid in place. Select the chunky function and leave to cook. Blend if you prefer. Season to taste if necessary. Serve as in step 4 above.

Cream of Fennel and Red Pepper Soup

Go for young bulbs of fennel, as fennel becomes tougher with age and then takes longer to cook.

Serves 2–4

1 large onion
2 fennel bulbs about 280 g/10 oz
1 red pepper
1 tbsp olive oil
Few drops of tabasco sauce
2 tsp lemon juice
700 ml/1 ¼ pints vegetable or chicken stock
Salt and freshly milled white pepper, to taste

Hot crusty bread, to serve

1. Finely chop the onion. Finely chop the fennel bulbs. Cut the pepper in half, remove the stalk and seeds and thinly slice.
2. *Blender-style soup maker* – Put the oil into the glass jar. Set the timer to 30 minutes and the temperature to high. Add the onion, cover and cook for 1 minute using the stir button occasionally. Add the fennel, cover and cook for 6–8 minutes until steaming, using the stir button occasionally.
3. Remove the lid and add the remaining ingredients. Cover, stir to mix and bring to the boil for 3–4 minutes, then reduce the heat to simmer and cook for the remaining time using the stir button occasionally. Blend until smooth.
4. If necessary, season to taste. Ladle or pour the piping hot soup into bowls. Serve immediately with hot crusty bread.

Jug-style soup maker
Put all the prepared ingredients (step 1 above) and other ingredients into the metal jug. (The level of total ingredients must be above the minimum mark and below the maximum.) Secure the lid in place. Select the purée function and leave to cook. Season to taste if necessary. Serve the soup as in step 4 above.

Prawn and Tomato Soup

Tomato with prawns, plus fish sauce and parsley – sounds like supper.

Serves 2–4

6 spring onions
400 g/14 oz ripe tomatoes
Small bunch of parsley
1 tbsp olive oil
1 tbsp lemon juice
2 tbsp fish sauce
700 ml/1 ¼ pints vegetable or chicken stock
280 g/10 oz cooked peeled prawns
Salt and freshly milled black pepper, to taste

Yogurt, to serve

1. Thinly slice the spring onions. Chop the tomatoes. Finely chop the parsley.
2. *Blender-style soup maker* – Put the oil into the glass jar. Set the timer to 20 minutes and the temperature to high. Add the spring onions, cover and cook for 2–3 minutes until steaming, using the stir button occasionally.
3. Remove the lid and add the remaining ingredients except the prawns. Cover, stir to mix and bring to the boil, then reduce the heat to simmer and cook for 10 minutes using the stir button occasionally. Add the prawns and cook for the remaining time using the stir button occasionally. Blend to the consistency you prefer. If necessary, season to taste. Ladle or spoon the piping hot soup into bowls. Top with a little yogurt and serve immediately.

Jug-style soup maker
Thaw the prawns if frozen.

Put all the prepared ingredients (step 1 above) and the other ingredients into the metal jug. (The level of total ingredients must be above the minimum mark and below the maximum.) Secure the lid in place. Select the purée function and leave to cook. Season to taste if necessary. Serve the soup as in step 3 above.

Chilli Bean Soup

A perennial favourite, red kidney beans with chilli the Mexican way.

Serves 2–4

1 medium onion
1 garlic clove
2 carrots
1 celery stalk
1 small potato
1 red chilli (see page 17)
400 g can red kidney beans
1 tbsp olive oil
700 ml/1 ¼ pints vegetable or chicken stock
400 g can tomatoes
2 tsp dried oregano
Salt and freshly milled black pepper, to taste

Grated Parmesan cheese and tortilla chips, to serve

1. Finely chop the onion and garlic. Cut the carrots into small pieces and thinly slice the celery. Cut the potato into small pieces. Cut the chilli in half, remove the stalk and seeds and thinly slice. Drain the kidney beans.
2. *Blender-style soup maker* – Put the oil into the glass jar. Set the timer to 30 minutes and the temperature to high. Add the onion and garlic, cover and cook for 1 minute using the stir button occasionally. Add the potato, carrots and celery, cover and cook for 5–6 minutes until steaming, using the stir button occasionally.
3. Remove the lid and add the remaining ingredients. Cover, stir to mix and bring to the boil for 3–4 minutes, then reduce the heat to simmer and cook for the remaining time using the stir button occasionally. Blend the soup to the consistency you prefer.
4. If necessary, season to taste. Ladle or pour the piping hot soup into bowls. Top with a little Parmesan cheese and serve immediately with tortilla chips.

Jug-style soup maker
Put all the prepared ingredients (step 1 above) and other ingredients, into the metal jug. (The level of total ingredients must be above the minimum mark and below the maximum.) Secure the lid in place. Select the chunky function and leave to cook. Blend the soup to the consistency you prefer. Season to taste if necessary. Serve the soup as in step 4 above.

Cabbage and Flageolet Bean Soup

Flageolets are young haricot beans, delicate pale green in colour.

Serves 2–4

1 medium onion
1 carrot
About 250 g/9 oz cabbage
400 g can flageolet beans
1 tbsp olive oil
700 ml/1 ¼ pints vegetable or chicken stock
400 g can tomatoes
2 tbsp tomato purée
2 tsp dried mixed herbs
Salt and freshly milled black pepper, to taste

Olive oil, to serve

1. Finely chop the onion. Cut the carrot into small pieces. Thinly slice the cabbage. Drain the flageolet beans.
2. *Blender-style soup maker* – Put the oil into the glass jar. Set the timer to 30 minutes and the temperature to high. Add the onion, cover and cook for 1 minute using the stir button occasionally. Add the carrot, cover and cook for 3–4 minutes until steaming, using the stir button occasionally.
3. Remove the lid and add the remaining ingredients. Cover, stir to mix and bring to the boil for 3–4 minutes, then reduce the heat to simmer and cook for the remaining time using the stir button occasionally. Blend the soup to the consistency you prefer.
4. If necessary, season to taste. Ladle or pour the piping hot soup into bowls. Top with a drizzle of olive oil and serve immediately.

Jug-style soup maker
Put all the prepared ingredients (step 1 above) and other ingredients into the metal jug. (The level of total ingredients must be above the minimum mark and below the maximum.) Secure the lid in place. Select the chunky function and leave to cook. Blend the soup to the consistency you prefer. Season to taste if necessary. Serve the soup as in step 4 above.

Creamy Tomato and Basil Soup

Sun-dried tomatoes give concentrated depth of flavour to this creamy soup.

Serves 2–3

1 large red onion
1 garlic clove
2 carrots
6 sun-dried tomatoes
Small bunch of basil
1 tbsp olive oil
½ tsp sugar
400g can tomatoes
700 ml/1 ¼ pints vegetable or chicken stock
150 ml/ ¼ pint double cream
Salt and freshly milled black pepper, to taste

Basil leaves, olive oil, to serve

1. Finely chop the onion and garlic. Chop the carrots into small pieces. Finely chop the sun-dried tomatoes. Pull the basil leaves from the stalks.
2. *Blender-style soup maker* – Put the oil into the glass jar. Set the timer to 25 minutes and the temperature to high. Add the onion and garlic, cover and cook for 1 minute using the stir button occasionally. Add the carrot, cover and cook for 4–5 minutes until steaming, using the stir button occasionally.
3. Remove the lid and add the remaining ingredients except the cream. Cover, stir to mix and bring to the boil, then reduce the heat to simmer and cook for the remaining time using the stir button occasionally. Blend to the consistency you prefer. Add the cream and blend a second.
4. If necessary, season to taste. Ladle or pour the piping hot soup into bowls. Top with basil leaves and a drizzle of olive oil. Serve immediately with hot garlic bread.

Jug-style soup maker
Put all the prepared ingredients (step 1 above) and other ingredients except the cream into the metal jug. (The level of total ingredients must be above the minimum mark and below the maximum.) Secure the lid in place. Select the chunky function and leave to cook. Blend to the consistency you prefer. Add the cream and blend a second. Season to taste if necessary. Serve as in step 4 above.

Green Pepper Soup

Green peppers are less sweet than the other colours, and are just right for this soup.

Serves 2–4

1 potato
1 medium leek
2 green peppers
1 tbsp olive oil
2 tbsp chopped coriander
700 ml/1 ¼ pints chicken or vegetable stock
Salt and freshly milled black pepper, to taste

Coriander leaves, to serve

1. Chop the potato into small pieces and thinly slice the leek. Cut the green peppers in half, remove the stalks and seeds and cut into small pieces.
2. *Blender-style soup maker* – Put the oil into the glass jar. Set the timer to 25 minutes and the temperature to high. Add the potato, leek and green pepper slices, cover and cook for 5–6 minutes until steaming, using the stir button occasionally.
3. Remove the lid and add the remaining ingredients. Cover, stir to mix and bring to the boil for 2 minutes, then reduce the heat to simmer and cook for the remaining time using the stir button occasionally. Blend the soup to the consistency you prefer.
4. If necessary, season to taste. Ladle or spoon the piping hot soup into bowls. Top with coriander leaves and serve immediately.

Jug-style soup maker
Put all the prepared ingredients (step 1 above) and other ingredients into the metal jug. (The level of total ingredients must be above the minimum mark and below the maximum.) Secure the lid in place. Select the purée function and leave to cook. Season to taste if necessary. Serve the soup as in step 4 above.

Broccoli, Celery and Sorrel Soup

Cauliflower would work as well as broccoli.

Serves 2–4

1 medium onion
1 celery heart
400 g/14 oz broccoli florets
2 large handfuls of sorrel leaves
1 tbsp sunflower oil
4 tomatoes
150 ml/¼ pint milk
700 ml/1 ¼ pints chicken or vegetable stock
Salt and freshly milled black pepper, to taste

Herb leaves, to serve

1. Finely chop the onion. Thinly slice or chop the celery heart. If large, roughly cut the broccoli florets into smaller pieces. Shred the sorrel leaves.
2. *Blender-style soup maker* – Put the oil into the glass jar. Set the timer to 30 minutes and the temperature to high. Add the onion, cover and cook for 1–2 minutes until beginning to steam using the stir button occasionally. Add the celery and broccoli florets, cover and cook for 4–5 minutes until beginning to steam using the stir button occasionally.
3. Remove the lid and add the remaining ingredients. Cover, stir to mix and bring to the boil for 2 minutes. Reduce the heat to simmer and cook for the remaining time using the stir button occasionally. Blend to the consistency you prefer.
4. If necessary, season to taste. Ladle or spoon the piping hot soup into bowls, top with herb leaves and serve immediately.

Jug-style soup maker
Put all the prepared ingredients (step 1 above) and other ingredients into the metal jug. (The level of total ingredients must be above the minimum mark and below the maximum.) Secure the lid in place. Select the chunky function and leave to cook. Blend to the consistency you prefer. Season to taste if necessary. Serve the soup as in step 4 above.

3

SOUP FIESTA

Another tantalizing mix of hot savoury soups. Some of them have just a little bit more spice. Feel confident and bold in searching out a soup to suit your mood or match the occasion. With plenty of rich and subtle flavours to work with, you can always increase the spice quota if you're feeling really exuberant.

Curried Parsnip and Carrot Soup

Coconut milk makes this a silky, velvety soup. Use a hotter curry paste if you dare.

Serves 2–4

1 small onion
1 garlic clove
2 parsnips
2 carrots
1 tbsp sunflower oil
2 tbsp mild curry paste
3 tbsp freshly chopped coriander
150 ml/¼ pint coconut milk
700 ml/1¼ pints vegetable or chicken stock
Salt and freshly milled black pepper, to taste

Natural yogurt and a few coriander leaves, to serve

1. Finely chop the onion and garlic. Roughly chop the parsnips and carrots into small pieces.
2. *Blender-style soup maker* – Put the oil into the glass jar. Set the timer to 30 minutes and the temperature to high. Add the onion and garlic, cover and cook for 1–2 minutes using the stir button occasionally until it begins to steam, but without browning too much. Add the parsnips and carrots, cover, stir and cook for 2 minutes.
3. Add the remaining ingredients. Cover, stir to mix and bring to the boil for 2 minutes. Reduce the heat to simmer and cook for the remaining time using the stir button occasionally. Blend to the consistency you prefer. If necessary, season to taste.
4. Ladle or pour the piping hot soup into bowls. Spoon yogurt on top and scatter over the coriander leaves. Serve immediately.

Jug-style soup maker
Put all the prepared ingredients (step 1 above) and other ingredients into the metal jug. (The level of total ingredients must be above the minimum mark and below the maximum.) Secure the lid in place. Select the purée function and leave to cook. Season to taste, if necessary, and serve the soup as in step 4 above.

Spiced Parsnip and Apple Soup

A fine soup for a cold winter's day.

Serves 2–4

1 medium red onion
2 medium parsnips
2 dessert apples
1 red chilli (see page 17)
Small piece of fresh root ginger
1 tbsp olive oil
700 ml/1 ¼ pints chicken or vegetable stock
1 tbsp chopped parsley
Salt and freshly milled black pepper, to taste

Chopped parsley, to serve

1. Finely chop the onion. Roughly chop the parsnips into small pieces. Peel, core and thinly slice the apples. Cut the chilli in half, remove the stalk and seeds and thinly slice. Finely grate the root ginger.
2. *Blender-style soup maker* – Put the oil into the glass jar. Set the timer to 30 minutes and the temperature to high. Add the onion, cover and cook for 1–2 minutes using the stir button occasionally until it begins to steam. Add the parsnips, cover, stir and cook for 4–5 minutes using the stir button occasionally until beginning to steam.
3. Add the remaining ingredients except the chopped parsley. Cover, stir to mix and bring to the boil for 2 minutes. Reduce the heat to simmer and cook for the remaining time using the stir button occasionally. Blend until smooth. Add the chopped parsley, cover and blend a second to mix. If necessary, season to taste.
4. Ladle or pour the piping hot soup into bowls. Sprinkle over a little parsley and serve immediately.

Jug-style soup maker
Put all the prepared ingredients except the chopped parsley (step 1 above) and other ingredients into the metal jug. (The level of total ingredients must be above the minimum mark and below the maximum.) Secure the lid in place. Select the purée function and leave to cook. Add the chopped parsley, cover and blend for a second. Season to taste, if necessary, and serve the soup as in step 4 above.

Sweet Potato, Fennel and Onion Soup

Sweet potato with its warm orangey colour gives a hint of sweetness and a smooth texture.

Serves 2–4

1 large onion
2 garlic cloves
2 sweet potatoes, about 250 g/9 oz each
1 small fennel bulb
1 tbsp olive oil
2 tbsp unsweetened orange juice
700 ml/1 ¼ pints vegetable or chicken stock
Salt and freshly milled white pepper, to taste

Fennel leaves and toasted sesame seeds, to serve

1. Finely chop the onion and crush the garlic. Chop the sweet potatoes into small pieces. Finely chop the fennel bulb.
2. *Blender-style soup maker* – Put the oil into the glass jar. Set the timer to 30 minutes and the temperature to high. Add the onion and garlic, cover and cook for 1 minute using the stir button occasionally. Add the sweet potato and fennel, cover and cook for 3–5 minutes until steaming, using the stir button occasionally.
3. Remove the lid and add the remaining ingredients. Cover, stir to mix and bring to the boil for 2–3 minutes, then reduce the heat to simmer and cook for the remaining time using the stir button occasionally. Blend to the consistency you prefer.
4. If necessary, season to taste. Ladle or pour the piping hot soup into bowls. Serve topped with fennel leaves and a sprinkling of sesame seeds. Serve immediately.

Jug-style soup maker
Put all the prepared ingredients (step 1 above) and other ingredients into the metal jug. (The level of total ingredients must be above the minimum mark and below the maximum.) Secure the lid in place. Select the chunky function and leave to cook. Blend to the consistency you prefer and season to taste, if necessary. Serve the soup as in step 4 above.

Carrot and Coconut Soup

A Thai element to this soup from the coriander and the coconut.

Serves 2–4

1 onion
450 g/1 lb carrots
Small bunch of coriander
1 tbsp olive oil
150 ml/¼ pint passata
400 ml can coconut milk
600 ml/1 pint vegetable or chicken stock
Salt and freshly milled black pepper, to taste

Toasted pine nuts, to serve

1. Finely chop the onion. Thinly slice the carrots. Pull the coriander leaves from the stalks and roughly chop.
2. *Blender-style soup maker* – Put the oil into the glass jar. Set the timer to 30 minutes and the temperature to high. Add the onion, cover and cook for 1–2 minutes using the stir button occasionally until beginning to brown a little. Add the carrots, cover and cook for 5–6 minutes using the stir button occasionally until beginning to steam.
3. Remove the lid and add the remaining ingredients. Cover, stir to mix and bring to the boil. Reduce the heat to simmer and cook for the remaining time using the stir button occasionally. Blend until smooth.
4. If necessary, season to taste. Ladle or pour the piping hot soup into bowls. Scatter over a few pine nuts and serve immediately.

Jug-style soup maker
Put all the prepared ingredients (step 1 above) and other ingredients into the metal jug. (The level of total ingredients must be above the minimum mark and below the maximum.) Secure the lid in place. Select the purée function and leave to cook. Season to taste if necessary. Serve as in step 4 above.

Spiced Sweet Potato Soup with Carrots

Spice mixes like five spice powder are tried and tested shortcuts to successful flavouring.

Serves 2–4

2 sweet potatoes, about 250 g/9 oz each
2 carrots
1 tbsp olive oil
½ tsp five spice powder
150 ml/¼ pint unsweetened orange juice
700 ml/1¼ pints vegetable or chicken stock
Salt and freshly milled black pepper, to taste

Hot crusty bread, to serve

1. Chop the sweet potatoes and carrots into small pieces.
2. *Blender-style soup maker* – Put the oil into the glass jar. Set the timer to 30 minutes and the temperature to high. Add the sweet potatoes and carrots, cover and cook for 6 minutes until steaming using the stir button occasionally.
3. Remove the lid and add the remaining ingredients. Cover, stir to mix and bring to the boil for 2–3 minutes, then reduce the heat to simmer and cook for the remaining time using the stir button occasionally. Blend to the consistency you prefer.
4. If necessary, season to taste. Ladle or pour the piping hot soup into bowls. Serve immediately with hot crusty bread.

Jug-style soup maker
Put all the prepared ingredients (step 1 above) and other ingredients into the metal jug. (The level of total ingredients must be above the minimum mark and below the maximum.) Secure the lid in place. Select the chunky function and leave to cook. Blend to the consistency you prefer and season to taste, if necessary. Serve the soup as in step 4 above.

Herby Garlic Mushroom Soup

Always a winner if you like garlic, which I certainly do.

Serves 2–4

1 medium onion
1 garlic clove
400 g/14 oz chestnut or button mushrooms
2 tbsp olive oil
300 ml/½ pint vegetable stock
300 ml/½ pint milk
150 ml/¼ pint dry white wine or vermouth, optional or use extra milk
  or stock
2 tbsp chopped mixed herbs – parsley, chives, dill or fennel
150 ml/¼ pint double cream
Salt and freshly milled white pepper, to taste

Chopped herbs, to serve

1. Finely chop the onion and garlic. Slice the mushrooms.
2. *Blender-style soup maker* – Put the oil into the glass jar. Set the timer to 20 minutes and the temperature to high. Add the onion and garlic, cover and cook for 1–2 minutes using the stir button occasionally until steaming, but without browning too much. Add the mushrooms, cover, stir and cook for 2 minutes.
3. Add the remaining ingredients except the cream. Cover, stir to mix and bring to the boil. Reduce the heat to simmer and cook for the remaining time using the stir button occasionally. Pour in the cream, cover and blend to the consistency you prefer. If necessary, season to taste.
4. Ladle or pour the piping hot soup into bowls. Scatter over chopped herbs and serve immediately.

Jug-style soup maker
Put all the prepared ingredients (step 1 above) and other ingredients except the cream into the metal jug. (The level of total ingredients must be above the minimum mark and below the maximum.) Secure the lid in place. Select the purée function and leave to cook. Add the cream, replace the lid and blend for a second. Season to taste, if necessary, and serve the soup as in step 4 above.

Creamy Cauliflower and Chorizo Soup

Spicy Spanish sausage is a perfect partner for cheesy, creamy cauliflower.

Serves 2–4

1 medium potato
500 g/1 lb 2 oz cauliflower florets
About 140 g/5 oz chorizo sausage
1 tbsp sunflower oil
600 ml/1 pint chicken or vegetable stock
1 tbsp chopped parsley
300 ml/ ½ pint milk
60 g/2 ¼ oz cream cheese
Salt and freshly milled black pepper, to taste

Grated cheese, to serve

1. Cut the potato into small pieces. If large, roughly cut the cauliflower florets into smaller pieces. Cut the chorizo sausage into small pieces.
2. Whilst the soup is cooking, dry-fry the chorizo in a pan until piping hot and cooked through.
3. *Blender-style soup maker* – Set the timer to 30 minutes and the temperature to high. Add all the ingredients except the chorizo sausage. Cover, stir and bring to the boil for 2–3 minutes, then reduce the heat to simmer and cook for the remaining time using the stir button occasionally. Leave chunky or blend as you prefer.
4. If necessary, season to taste. Add the piping hot chorizo sausage and stir to mix. Ladle or spoon the piping hot soup into bowls, sprinkle over a little grated cheese and serve immediately.

Jug-style soup maker
Cook the chorizo sausage (see step 2 above).

Put all the prepared ingredients except the chorizo sausage (step 1 above) and other ingredients into the metal jug. (The level of total ingredients must be above the minimum mark and below the maximum.) Secure the lid in place. Select the purée function and leave to cook. Add the piping hot chorizo sausage and blend for a second to mix. Season to taste if necessary. Serve the soup as in step 4 above.

Spinach and Coconut Soup

A simple soup with a bit of a kick from the cayenne pepper.

Serves 2–4

2 onions
1 garlic clove
1 large potato
250 g/9 oz spinach leaves
1 tbsp olive oil
¼ tsp cayenne pepper
200 ml can coconut milk
700 ml/1 ¼ pints vegetable or chicken stock
Salt and freshly milled black pepper, to taste

Cream or yogurt and lime wedges, to serve

1. Finely chop the onions and crush the garlic. Cut the potato into small pieces. Thinly slice the spinach leaves, if large.
2. *Blender-style soup maker* – Put the oil into the glass jar. Set the timer to 20 minutes and the temperature to high. Add the onion and garlic, cover and cook for 1–2 minutes using the stir button occasionally until beginning to steam, but without browning too much. Add the potato, cover and cook for 3–4 minutes using the stir button occasionally until beginning to steam.
3. Remove the lid and add the remaining ingredients. Cover, stir to mix and bring to the boil. Reduce the heat to simmer and cook for the remaining time using the stir button occasionally. Blend until smooth.
4. If necessary, season to taste. Ladle or pour the piping hot soup into bowls. Swirl over a little cream or yogurt and serve immediately with lime wedges on the side.

Jug-style soup maker
Put all the prepared ingredients (step 1 above) and other ingredients into the metal jug. (The level of total ingredients must be above the minimum mark and below the maximum.) Secure the lid in place. Select the purée function and leave to cook. Season to taste if necessary. Serve as in step 4 above.

Turnip and Mustard Soup

Too often overlooked, turnip is an adaptable vegetable. Look out for the smaller varieties.

Serves 2–4

1 onion
1 medium turnip about 300 g/10 ½ oz
1 medium potato
1 tbsp olive oil
2–3 tbsp wholegrain mustard
700 ml/1 ¼ pints vegetable stock
Salt and freshly milled black pepper, to taste

Hot bread, to serve

1. Finely chop the onion. Roughly chop the turnip and potato into small pieces.
2. *Blender-style soup maker* – Put the oil into the glass jar. Set the timer to 30 minutes and the temperature to high. Add the onion, cover and cook for 1–2 minutes using the stir button occasionally until beginning to steam. Add the potato and turnip, cover, stir and cook for 3–4 minutes using the stir button occasionally until beginning to steam.
3. Add the remaining ingredients. Cover, stir to mix and bring to the boil for 2 minutes. Reduce the heat to simmer and cook for the remaining time using the stir button occasionally. Blend until smooth and, if necessary, season to taste.
4. Ladle or pour the piping hot soup into bowls. Serve immediately with hot bread.

Jug-style soup maker
Put all the prepared ingredients (step 1 above) and other ingredients into the metal jug. (The level of total ingredients must be above the minimum mark and below the maximum.) Secure the lid in place. Select the purée function and leave to cook. Season to taste, if necessary, and serve the soup as in step 4 above.

Spiced Butternut Squash and Bacon Soup

Good substitutes for butternut squash would be sweet potato or marrow.

Serves 2–4

1 onion
2 garlic cloves
500 g/1 lb 2 oz wedge of butternut squash
1 medium potato
2 tbsp sunflower oil
Small bunch of fresh coriander
1–2 tsp mild curry paste
700 ml/1 ¼ pints vegetable or chicken stock
Salt and freshly milled black pepper, to taste

4 rashers streaky or back bacon

1. Finely chop the onion and garlic. Remove any seeds from the butternut squash, peel and cut into small cubes with the potato.
2. *Blender-style soup maker* – Put the oil into the glass jar. Set the timer to 30 minutes and the temperature to high. Add the onion and garlic, cover and cook for 1–2 minutes using the stir button occasionally until they begin to steam but without browning too much.
3. Remove the lid and add the remaining ingredients except the bacon. Cover, stir to mix and bring to the boil. Reduce the heat to simmer and cook for the remaining time using the stir button occasionally. Blend to the consistency you prefer. If necessary, season to taste.
4. Whilst the soup is cooking, grill the bacon rashers. Cut the rind off the bacon rashers. Put the rashers under a hot grill and cook on both sides until crispy. With scissors, cut into small pieces.
5. Ladle or pour the piping hot soup into bowls. Scatter over the hot bacon pieces and serve immediately.

Jug-style soup maker
Put all the prepared ingredients (step 1 above) and other ingredients except the bacon into the metal jug. (The level of total ingredients must be above the minimum mark and below the maximum.) Secure the lid in place. Select the purée function and leave to cook. Season to taste, if necessary. Grill the bacon rashers and serve the soup as in steps 4 and 5 above.

Mulligatawny Soup

A rich soupy broth flavoured with curry; you can add a little meat or chicken.

Serves 2–4

1 onion	1–2 tsp curry powder or paste,
2 garlic cloves	choose a favourite
2 carrots	1 tbsp mango chutney
1 small potato	3 tbsp chopped parsley
1 celery stick	700 ml/1 ¼ pints chicken stock
1 medium cooking apple	A few sultanas
2 handfuls of spinach leaves	Salt and freshly milled black pepper,
2 tbsp sunflower oil	to taste

Yogurt and hot naan bread, to serve

1. Finely chop the onion and garlic. Cut the carrots and potato into small pieces. Thinly slice the celery. Peel, core and chop the apple. Tear the spinach leaves in half, if large.
2. *Blender-style soup maker* – Put the oil into the glass jar. Set the timer to 30 minutes and the temperature to high. Add the onion and garlic, cover and cook for 1 minute using the stir button occasionally. Add the carrots, potato and celery, cover and cook for 5–6 minutes until steaming, using the stir button occasionally.
3. Remove the lid and add the remaining ingredients except the sultanas. Cover, stir to mix and bring to the boil, then reduce the heat to simmer and cook for the remaining time using the stir button occasionally. Leave the soup chunky or blend to the consistency you prefer. Add the sultanas and stir.
4. If necessary, season to taste. Ladle or pour the piping hot soup into bowls. Top with a blob of yogurt and serve immediately with hot naan bread.

Jug-style soup maker
Put all the prepared ingredients (step 1 above) and other ingredients except the sultanas into the metal jug. (The level of total ingredients must be above the minimum mark and below the maximum.) Secure the lid in place. Select the chunky function and leave to cook. Season to taste, if necessary, and blend to the consistency you prefer. Add the sultanas and blend for a second. Serve as in step 4 above.

Artichoke and Walnut Soup

Artichoke hearts have a nutty taste which nutmeg brings to the fore.

Serves 2–4

1 shallot
1 medium potato
400 g can artichoke hearts
1 tbsp olive oil
1 tbsp lemon juice
700 ml/1 ¼ pints vegetable or chicken stock
Large pinch of grated nutmeg
60 g/2 ¼ oz chopped walnuts
Salt and freshly milled black pepper, to taste

Walnut pieces and hot breadsticks, to serve

1. Finely chop the shallot. Chop the potato into small pieces. Drain the artichokes and roughly chop.
2. *Blender-style soup maker* – Put the oil into the glass jar. Set the timer to 25 minutes and the temperature to high. Add the shallot, cover and cook for 1–2 minutes until steaming but not browning, using the stir button occasionally. Remove the lid and add the remaining ingredients except the walnuts. Cover, stir to mix and bring to the boil for 3–4 minutes, then reduce the heat to simmer and cook for the remaining time using the stir button occasionally. Blend until smooth. Add the chopped walnuts and blend for a second.
3. If necessary, season to taste. Ladle or pour the piping hot soup into bowls. Top with walnut pieces. Serve immediately with hot breadsticks.

Jug-style soup maker
Put all the prepared ingredients (step 1 above) and other ingredients except the chopped walnuts into the metal jug. (The level of total ingredients must be above the minimum mark and below the maximum.) Secure the lid in place. Select the purée function and leave to cook. Add the chopped walnuts and blend for a second. Season to taste if necessary. Serve the soup as in step 3 above.

Thai Chicken and Red Chilli Soup

When using pastes like Thai green chilli, choose the best quality ones.

Serves 2–4

2 shallots
2 celery sticks
1 red chilli (see page 17)
150 g/5 ½ oz mushrooms
300 g/10 ½ oz boneless fresh chicken
1 tbsp olive oil
2 tbsp Thai green chilli paste
2 tbsp fish sauce
2 handfuls of small spinach leaves
700 ml/1 ¼ pints chicken stock
Salt and freshly milled black pepper, to taste

Lemon wedges and crusty bread, to serve

1. Finely chop the shallots. Thinly slice the celery sticks. Cut the chilli in half, remove the stalk and seeds and thinly slice. Roughly chop the mushrooms. Cut the chicken into small pieces.
2. *Blender-style soup maker* – Put the oil into the glass jar. Set the timer to 30 minutes and the temperature to simmer. Add the chicken, shallots and celery, cover and cook for 15–18 minutes until the chicken is cooked through using the stir button occasionally. Increase the heat to high.
3. Remove the lid and add the remaining ingredients. Cover, stir to mix and bring to the boil for 2 minutes. Reduce the heat to simmer and cook for the remaining time using the stir button occasionally. Blend until smooth.
4. If necessary, season to taste. Ladle or pour the piping hot soup into bowls. Serve immediately with lemon wedges and crusty bread.

Jug-style soup maker
Use cooked chicken, not raw.

Put all the prepared ingredients (step 1 above) and other ingredients into the metal jug. (The level of total ingredients must be above the minimum mark and below the maximum.) Secure the lid in place. Select the chunky function and leave to cook. Blend to the consistency you prefer. Season to taste if necessary. Serve as in step 4 above.

Salmon and Coconut Soup

A soup to share with your friends.

Serves 2–4

1 medium onion
2 carrots
1 small potato
300 g/10½ oz salmon fillet
Small bunch of parsley
1 tbsp olive oil
150 ml/¼ pint passata
400 ml can coconut milk
600 ml/1 pint vegetable or chicken stock
Salt and freshly milled black pepper, to taste

Parsley and toasted cashew nuts, to serve

1. Finely chop the onion. Thinly slice the carrots. Chop the potato into small pieces. Remove any skin and bones from the salmon and cut into small pieces. Pull the parsley leaves from the stalks and roughly chop.
2. *Blender-style soup maker* – Put the oil into the glass jar. Set the timer to 30 minutes and the temperature to high. Add the onion, cover and cook for 1–2 minutes using the stir button occasionally until beginning to brown a little. Add the carrots, potato and salmon, cover and cook for 5–6 minutes using the stir button occasionally until beginning to steam.
3. Remove the lid and add the remaining ingredients. Cover, stir to mix and bring to the boil. Reduce the heat to simmer and cook for the remaining time using the stir button occasionally. Blend until smooth.
4. If necessary, season to taste. Ladle or pour the piping hot soup into bowls. Top with a few cashew nuts and parsley and serve immediately.

Jug-style soup maker
Use cooked salmon fillet, not raw.

Put all the prepared ingredients (step 1 above) and other ingredients into the metal jug. (The level of total ingredients must be above the minimum mark and below the maximum.) Secure the lid in place. Select the purée function and leave to cook. Season to taste if necessary. Serve as in step 4 above.

Italian Red Pepper Soup with Bulgur Wheat

A sunshine burst of ingredients with a distinctly Italian feel.

Serves 2–4

1 onion
2 garlic cloves
2 red peppers
3–4 sprigs of oregano
6 stoned black olives
2 tbsp olive oil
400 g can chopped tomatoes
¼ tsp sugar
2 tbsp lemon juice
700 ml/1 ¼ pints chicken or vegetable stock
3 tbsp bulgur wheat
Salt and freshly milled black pepper, to taste

Oregano leaves and sliced olives, to serve

1. Finely chop the onion and crush the garlic. Cut the red peppers in half, remove the stalks and seeds and thinly slice. Pull the oregano leaves from the stalks. Thinly slice the black olives and put in a small bowl.
2. *Blender-style soup maker* – Put the oil into the glass jar. Set the timer to 30 minutes and the temperature to high. Add the onion and garlic, cover and cook for 1 minute using the stir button occasionally. Add the red pepper, cover and cook for 5 minutes until steaming, using the stir button occasionally.
3. Remove the lid and add the remaining ingredients except the olives and bulgur wheat. Cover, stir to mix and bring to the boil, then reduce the heat to simmer and cook for the remaining time using the stir button occasionally.
4. Whilst the soup is cooking, tip the bulgur wheat into a large bowl. Pour over boiling water to cover and leave until the soup is ready. Drain in a sieve and press with the back of a spoon to remove excess water.
5. Blend the soup to the consistency you prefer. Add the olives and the hot drained bulgur wheat and stir for 1–2 seconds to just mix in. If necessary, season to taste.
6. Ladle or spoon the piping hot soup into bowls and scatter over a few oregano leaves and olive slices. Serve immediately.

Jug-style soup maker
To soak the bulgur wheat follow step 4 above.

Put all the prepared ingredients (step 1 above) and other ingredients, except the olives and bulgur wheat, into the metal jug. (The level of total ingredients must be above the minimum mark and below the maximum.) Secure the lid in place. Select the chunky function and leave to cook. Leave chunky or blend as you prefer. Add the olives and bulgur wheat and blend to mix. Season to taste if necessary. Serve the soup as in step 6 above.

4

SOUP SELECTION

Soups can be a main meal. There are several to choose from among these recipes that will help you fill that hunger gap. Noodles, pasta and rice, lurking at the bottom of the soup bowl, are so plump and infused with flavour as they are eagerly spooned to the surface.

Lentil and Fennel Soup

A dhal-like soup, you could also serve it with an Indian bread.

Serves 2–4

1 medium leek
2 medium carrots
Large bunch of fennel leaves
1 tbsp sunflower oil
300 ml/½ pint milk
500 ml/18 fl oz vegetable or chicken stock
140 g/5 oz red split lentils
3 tbsp chopped coriander
Salt and freshly milled black pepper, to taste

Natural yogurt and fennel leaves, to serve

1. Thinly slice the leek and roughly chop the carrots into small cubes. Roughly chop the fennel leaves.
2. *Blender-style soup maker* – Put the oil into the glass jar. Set the timer to 30 minutes and the temperature to high. Add the sliced leek, cover and cook for 1–2 minutes using the stir button occasionally until it begins to steam, but without browning too much. Add the carrots, cover, stir and cook for 3 minutes, using the stir button occasionally, until they begin to steam.
3. Add the remaining ingredients except the chopped coriander. Cover, stir to mix and bring to the boil for 2 minutes. Reduce the heat to simmer and cook for the remaining time using the stir button occasionally. Blend to the consistency you prefer. Add the chopped coriander, cover and blend for a second. If necessary, season to taste.
4. Ladle or pour the piping hot soup into bowls. Top with fennel leaves and serve immediately.

Jug-style soup maker
Put all the prepared ingredients (step 1 above) and other ingredients, except the chopped coriander into the metal jug. (The level of total ingredients must be above the minimum mark and below the maximum.) Secure the lid in place. Select the purée function and leave to cook. Add the chopped coriander, cover and blend for a second. Season to taste, if necessary, and serve the soup as in step 4 above.

Creamy Mushroom and Bacon Soup

Other types of mushrooms could be used. Try a selection of wild mushrooms.

Serves 2–4

1 medium onion
1 garlic clove
400 g/14 oz chestnut or button mushrooms
2 tbsp olive oil
450 ml/16 fl oz chicken or vegetable stock
300 ml/½ pint milk
2 tbsp chopped mixed herbs – parsley, chives, dill or fennel
150 ml/¼ pint double cream
Salt and freshly milled white pepper, to taste
5 rashers streaky or back bacon

Croûtons (page 123), to serve

1. Finely chop the onion and garlic. Slice the mushrooms.
2. *Blender-style soup maker* – Put the oil into the glass jar. Set the timer to 20 minutes and the temperature to high. Add the onion and garlic, cover and cook for 1–2 minutes using the stir button occasionally until they begin to steam, but without browning too much. Add the mushrooms, cover, stir and cook for 2 minutes.
3. Add the remaining ingredients, except the cream and bacon. Cover, stir to mix and bring to the boil. Reduce the heat to simmer and cook for the remaining time using the stir button occasionally. Pour in the cream, cover and blend to the consistency you prefer. If necessary, season to taste.
4. Whilst the soup is cooking, grill the bacon rashers. Cut the rind off the bacon rashers. Put the rashers under a hot grill and cook on both sides until crispy. With scissors, cut into small pieces. Put the piping hot bacon pieces into the soup, cover and stir to mix.
5. Ladle or pour the piping hot soup into bowls. Scatter over the croûtons and serve immediately.

Jug-style soup maker
Put all the prepared ingredients (step 1 above) and other ingredients except the cream and bacon into the metal jug. (The level of total ingredients must be above the minimum mark and below the maximum.) Secure the lid in place. Select the purée function and leave to cook. Add the cream, replace the lid and blend for a second. Season to taste, if necessary. Grill the bacon rashers as in step 4 above and serve the soup as in step 5.

Lemon Minted Pea Soup with Leaves

Such a simple recipe to make – I'm sure we all have a bag of frozen peas lurking at the back of the freezer.

Serves 2–4

6 spring onions
Large handful of Chinese leaves
Small bunch of watercress
1 tbsp light soy sauce
2 tbsp lemon juice
500 g/1 lb 2 oz minted peas, frozen or fresh
850 ml/1 ½ pints chicken or vegetable stock
Salt and freshly milled black pepper, to taste

Lemon slices and sesame seed oil, to serve

1. Thinly slice the spring onions. Thinly slice the Chinese leaves. Pull the watercress leaves from the stalks.
2. *Blender-style soup maker* – Set the timer to 18 minutes and the temperature to high. Add all the ingredients, cover, stir and bring to the boil for 2–3 minutes, then reduce the heat to simmer and cook for the remaining time using the stir button occasionally. Leave chunky, although blend if you prefer.
3. If necessary, season to taste. Ladle or pour the piping hot soup into bowls topped with a lemon slice and a few drops of sesame seed oil sprinkled on top. Serve immediately.

Jug-style soup maker
Thaw the peas if frozen.

Put all the prepared ingredients (step 1 above) and other ingredients into the metal jug. (The level of total ingredients must be above the minimum mark and below the maximum.) Secure the lid in place. Select the chunky function and leave to cook. Leave chunky, although blend if you prefer. Season to taste if necessary. Serve the soup as in step 3 above.

Asparagus and Mushroom Soup

An elegant soup, one to impress your friends.

Serves 2–4

1 medium onion
350 g/12 oz wild, chestnut or button mushrooms
250 g/9 oz asparagus
2 tbsp olive oil
2 tbsp lemon juice
700 ml/1 ¼ pints vegetable or chicken stock
150 ml/¼ pint dry white wine or vermouth, optional or use extra stock
4 tbsp chopped parsley
Salt and freshly milled white pepper, to taste

Parsley sprigs, to serve

1. Finely chop the onion. Slice the mushrooms. Trim and discard any woody ends from the asparagus spears. Cut each spear into 3 or 4 pieces.
2. *Blender-style soup maker* – Put the oil into the glass jar. Set the timer to 20 minutes and the temperature to high. Add the onion, cover and cook for 1–2 minutes using the stir button occasionally until it begins to steam, but without browning too much. Add the mushrooms, cover, stir and cook for 2 minutes.
3. Add the remaining ingredients. Cover, stir to mix and bring to the boil. Reduce the heat to simmer and cook for the remaining time using the stir button occasionally. Blend to the consistency you prefer. If necessary, season to taste.
4. Ladle or pour the piping hot soup into bowls. Top with parsley sprigs and serve immediately.

Jug-style soup maker
Put all the prepared ingredients (step 1 above) and other ingredients into the metal jug. (The level of total ingredients must be above the minimum mark and below the maximum.) Secure the lid in place. Select the purée function and leave to cook. Season to taste, if necessary, and serve the soup as in step 4 above.

Carrot, Tomato and Ginger Soup

Cartons or bottles of passata are useful store-cupboard ingredients. Ginger adds zest and spice.

Serves 2–4

1 medium red onion
4 carrots
5 cm/2 inch piece of root ginger
2 tsp vegetable oil
½ tsp ground cumin
450 ml/16 fl oz passata or sieved tomatoes
300 ml/½ pint vegetable stock
¼ tsp sugar
Salt and freshly milled black pepper, to taste

Croûtons (page 123), to serve

1. Finely chop the onion. Roughly chop the carrots into small pieces. Grate the root ginger.
2. *Blender-style soup maker* – Put the oil into the glass jar. Set the timer to 30 minutes and the temperature to high. Add the onion, cover and cook for 1–2 minutes using the stir button occasionally until steaming, but without browning too much. Add the carrots, cover, stir and cook for 2 minutes.
3. Add the remaining ingredients. Cover, stir to mix and bring to the boil for 2 minutes. Reduce the heat to simmer and cook for the remaining time using the stir button occasionally. Blend to the consistency you prefer. If necessary, season to taste.
4. Ladle or pour the piping hot soup into bowls. Scatter over some croûtons and serve immediately.

Jug-style soup maker
Put all the prepared ingredients (step 1 above) and other ingredients into the metal jug. (The level of total ingredients must be above the minimum mark and below the maximum.) Secure the lid in place. Select the purée function and leave to cook. Season to taste, if necessary, and serve the soup as in step 4 above.

Root Vegetable Soup

A soup bonanza from the allotment.

Serves 2–4

1 medium red onion
1 small parsnip
1 mini-sized turnip
1 carrot
1 medium potato
1 tbsp olive oil
2 tbsp tomato purée
700 ml/1 ¼ pints vegetable stock
Salt and freshly milled black pepper, to taste

Chopped parsley, to serve

1. Finely chop the onion. Roughly chop the parsnip, turnip, carrot and potato into small pieces.
2. *Blender-style soup maker* – Put the oil into the glass jar. Set the timer to 30 minutes and the temperature to high. Add the onion, cover and cook for 1–2 minutes using the stir button occasionally until beginning to steam. Add the parsnip, turnip, carrot and potato. Cover, stir and cook for 4–5 minutes using the stir button occasionally until beginning to steam.
3. Add the remaining ingredients. Cover, stir to mix and bring to the boil for 2 minutes. Reduce the heat to simmer and cook for the remaining time using the stir button occasionally. Blend until smooth, and if necessary, season to taste.
4. Ladle or pour the piping hot soup into bowls. Sprinkle over a little parsley and serve immediately.

Jug-style soup maker
Put all the prepared ingredients (step 1 above) and other ingredients into the metal jug. (The level of total ingredients must be above the minimum mark and below the maximum.) Secure the lid in place. Select the purée function and leave to cook. Season to taste, if necessary, and serve the soup as in step 4 above.

Fennel, Apple and Celery Soup

A great combination of flavours.

Serves 2–4

1 large onion
1 fennel bulb about 140 g/5 oz
2 celery sticks
2 eating apples
1 tbsp olive oil
700 ml/1 ¼ pints vegetable or chicken stock
Salt and freshly milled white pepper, to taste

Chopped toasted hazelnut pieces, to serve

1. Finely chop the onion. Finely chop the fennel bulb. Thinly slice the celery sticks. Peel, core and chop the apples.
2. *Blender-style soup maker* – Put the oil into the glass jar. Set the timer to 30 minutes and the temperature to high. Add the onion, cover and cook for 1 minute using the stir button occasionally. Add the fennel and celery, cover and cook for 5–6 minutes until steaming, using the stir button occasionally.
3. Remove the lid and add the remaining ingredients. Cover, stir to mix and bring to the boil for 3–4 minutes, then reduce the heat to simmer and cook for the remaining time using the stir button occasionally. Blend until smooth.
4. If necessary, season to taste. Ladle or pour the piping hot soup into bowls. Sprinkle over a few hazelnut pieces and serve immediately.

Jug-style soup maker
Put all the prepared ingredients (step 1 above) and other ingredients into the metal jug. (The level of total ingredients must be above the minimum mark and below the maximum.) Secure the lid in place. Select the purée function and leave to cook. Season to taste if necessary. Serve the soup as in step 4 above.

Pasta and Ham Soup with Herbs

I've used fresh pasta for speed. You can use dried, but allow extra cooking time.

Serves 2–4

2 medium onions
1 celery stick
1 large bunch of mixed herbs, chives, parsley, oregano, thyme
250 g/9 oz piece of cooked lean ham
1 tbsp olive oil
1 tsp maple syrup or clear honey
850 ml/1 ½ pints ham or vegetable stock
300 g/10 ½ oz fresh pasta shapes, such as spirals, shells
Salt and freshly milled black pepper, to taste

Olive oil, to serve

1. Finely chop the onions. Thinly slice the celery stick. Pull the herb leaves from the stalks and finely chop. Cut the ham into small pieces.
2. *Blender-style soup maker* – Put the oil into the glass jar. Set the timer to 30 minutes and the temperature to high. Add the onion and celery, cover, stir to mix and cook for 5–6 minutes until beginning to steam using the stir button occasionally.
3. Remove the lid and add the remaining ingredients except the ham and pasta. Cover, stir to mix and bring to the boil for 2 minutes. Reduce the heat to simmer and cook for 8–10 minutes. Add the ham, cover and cook for the remaining time using the stir button occasionally.
4. Whilst the soup is cooking, cook the pasta following the packet instructions. Blend the soup to the consistency you prefer.
5. If necessary, season to taste. Spoon the piping hot pasta into soup bowls. Ladle or pour the piping hot soup over. Drizzle over a little oil and serve immediately.

Jug-style soup maker
To cook the pasta follow step 4 above.

Put all the prepared ingredients (step 1 above) and other ingredients except the pasta into the metal jug. (The level of total ingredients must be above the minimum mark and below the maximum.) Secure the lid in place. Select the chunky function and leave to cook. Blend to the consistency you prefer. Season to taste if necessary. Serve as in step 5 above.

Broccoli and Cream Cheese Soup

A lovely swirl through the soup of creamy cheese, flavoured with herbs.

Serves 2–4

1 medium onion
1 small potato
400 g/14 oz broccoli florets
125 g/4 ½ oz low-fat cream cheese with herbs
1 tbsp chopped parsley
150 ml/ ¼ pint milk
1 tbsp sunflower oil
700 ml/1 ¼ pints chicken or vegetable stock
Salt and freshly milled black pepper, to taste

Herb leaves, to serve

1. Finely chop the onion. Cut the potato into small pieces. If large, roughly cut the broccoli florets into smaller pieces. Spoon the cream cheese into a small bowl and stir in the chopped parsley and a little of the milk to soften the mix.
2. *Blender-style soup maker* – Put the oil into the glass jar. Set the timer to 30 minutes and the temperature to high. Add the onion, cover, and cook for 1–2 minutes until beginning to steam using the stir button occasionally. Add the potato and broccoli florets, cover and cook for 4–5 minutes until beginning to steam using the stir button occasionally.
3. Remove the lid and add the remaining ingredients except the cream cheese mixture. Cover, stir to mix and bring to the boil for 2 minutes. Reduce the heat to simmer and cook for the remaining time using the stir button occasionally. Blend until smooth. Add the cream cheese mix and blend for a second.
4. If necessary, season to taste. Ladle or spoon the piping hot soup into bowls, top with herb leaves and serve immediately.

Jug-style soup maker
Put all the prepared ingredients (step 1 above) and other ingredients except the cream cheese mixture into the metal jug. (The level of total ingredients must be above the minimum mark and below the maximum.) Secure the lid in place. Select the purée function and leave to cook. Add the cream cheese mix and blend for a second to mix. Season to taste if necessary. Serve the soup as in step 4 above.

Courgette, Tomato and Red Pepper Soup

The flavour of orange works well with tomatoes and red peppers.

Serves 2–4

1 large red onion
2 garlic cloves
2 medium red peppers
2 medium courgettes
Small bunch of basil
1 tbsp olive oil
Pinch of sugar
400 g can tomatoes
150 ml/ ¼ pint unsweetened orange juice
600 ml/1 pint chicken or vegetable stock
Salt and freshly milled black pepper, to taste

Basil leaves and crusty bread, to serve

1. Finely chop the onion and crush the garlic. Cut the red peppers in half, remove the stalks and seeds and thinly slice. Dice the courgettes and pull the leaves from the basil.
2. *Blender-style soup maker* – Put the oil into the glass jar. Set the timer to 30 minutes and the temperature to high. Add the onion and garlic, cover and cook for 1 minute using the stir button occasionally. Add the red pepper and courgettes, cover and cook for 3–4 minutes until steaming, using the stir button occasionally.
3. Remove the lid and add the remaining ingredients. Cover, stir to mix and bring to the boil, then reduce the heat to simmer and cook for the remaining time using the stir button occasionally. Blend to the consistency you prefer.
4. If necessary, season to taste. Ladle or pour the piping hot soup into bowls. Top with basil leaves and serve immediately with crusty bread.

Jug-style soup maker
Put all the prepared ingredients (step 1 above) and other ingredients into the metal jug. (The level of total ingredients must be above the minimum mark and below the maximum.) Secure the lid in place. Select the chunky function and leave to cook. Blend to the consistency you prefer. Season to taste, if necessary, and serve as in step 4 above.

Fennel, Courgette and Borlotti Bean Soup

A hearty soup with Italian pesto and borlotti beans.

Serves 2–4

1 medium onion
2 small courgettes
1 small fennel bulb
400 g can borlotti beans
1 tbsp olive oil
700 ml/1 ¼ pints vegetable or chicken stock
400 g can tomatoes
1 tbsp tomato pesto
Salt and freshly milled black pepper, to taste

Flakes of Parmesan cheese, to serve

1. Finely chop the onion. Cut the courgettes into small pieces. Chop the fennel into small pieces. Drain the borlotti beans.
2. *Blender-style soup maker* – Put the oil into the glass jar. Set the timer to 30 minutes and the temperature to high. Add the onion, cover and cook for 1 minute using the stir button occasionally. Add the courgettes, cover and cook for 3–4 minutes until steaming, using the stir button occasionally.
3. Remove the lid and add the remaining ingredients. Cover, stir to mix and bring to the boil for 3–4 minutes, then reduce the heat to simmer and cook for the remaining time using the stir button occasionally. Blend the soup to the consistency you prefer.
4. If necessary, season to taste. Ladle or pour the piping hot soup into bowls. Top with flakes of Parmesan cheese and serve immediately.

Jug-style soup maker
Put all the prepared ingredients (step 1 above) and other ingredients, into the metal jug. (The level of total ingredients must be above the minimum mark and below the maximum.) Secure the lid in place. Select the chunky function and leave to cook. Blend the soup to the consistency you prefer. Season to taste if necessary. Serve the soup as in step 4 above.

Sausage, Spinach and Chickpea Soup

Could be a main meal; use your favourite type of sausage.

Serves 2–4

1 medium onion	1 tbsp olive oil
1 garlic clove	700 ml/1 ¼ pints vegetable or
2 carrots	chicken stock
1 celery stick	400 g can tomatoes
400 g can chickpeas	4 tbsp tomato ketchup
1 large handful of spinach leaves	Salt and freshly milled black pepper,
8 butcher's sausages	to taste

Hot garlic bread, to serve

1. Finely chop the onion and garlic. Cut the carrots into small pieces and thinly slice the celery. Drain the chickpeas. Thinly slice the spinach leaves. Cut each sausage into four pieces.
2. *Blender-style soup maker* – Put the oil into the glass jar. Set the timer to 30 minutes and the temperature to high. Add the onion and garlic, cover and cook for 1 minute using the stir button occasionally. Add the carrots and celery, cover and cook for 5–6 minutes until steaming, using the stir button occasionally.
3. Remove the lid and add the remaining ingredients except the sausages. Cover, stir to mix and bring to the boil for 5–6 minutes, then reduce the heat to simmer and cook for the remaining time using the stir button occasionally.
4. Grill or fry the sausage pieces until cooked through and piping hot.
5. Blend the soup to the consistency you prefer.
6. If necessary, season to taste. Ladle or pour the piping hot soup into bowls and stir in the hot sausage pieces. Serve immediately with hot garlic bread.

Jug-style soup maker
Use piping hot cooked sausages.

Put all the prepared ingredients (step 1 above) and other ingredients except the sausage pieces, into the metal jug. (The level of total ingredients must be above the minimum mark and below the maximum.) Secure the lid in place. Select the chunky function and leave to cook. Grill or fry the sausage pieces (step 4 above). Blend the soup to the consistency you prefer. Season to taste if necessary. Serve the soup as in step 6 above.

Pea and Ham Soup

A traditional favourite. Make sure the ham stock isn't too salty.

Serves 2–4

2 medium onions
1 potato
250 g/9 oz piece of cooked lean ham
1 tbsp olive oil
500 g/1 lb 2 oz minted peas, frozen or fresh
2 tsp capers (optional)
1 tbsp chopped parsley
700 ml/1 ¼ pints ham or vegetable stock
Salt and freshly milled black pepper, to taste

Crusty bread, to serve

1. Finely chop the onions. Chop the potato into small pieces. Cut the ham into small pieces.
2. *Blender-style soup maker* – Put the oil into the glass jar. Set the timer to 30 minutes and the temperature to high. Add the onion, cover, stir to mix and cook for 2–3 minutes until beginning to steam using the stir button occasionally. Add the potato, cover and cook for 3–4 minutes until steaming, using the stir button occasionally.
3. Remove the lid and add the remaining ingredients except the ham. Cover, stir to mix and bring to the boil for 2 minutes. Reduce the heat to simmer and cook for 10 minutes. Add the ham, cover and cook for the remaining time using the stir button occasionally. Blend to the consistency you prefer.
4. If necessary, season to taste. Ladle or pour the piping hot soup into bowls. Serve immediately with crusty bread.

Jug-style soup maker
Thaw the peas if frozen.

   Put all the prepared ingredients (step 1 above) and other ingredients into the metal jug. (The level of total ingredients must be above the minimum mark and below the maximum.) Secure the lid in place. Select the chunky function and leave to cook. Blend to the consistency you prefer. Season to taste if necessary. Serve as in step 4 above.

Sorrel and Broad Bean Soup

Sorrel leaves have a fresh lemon flavour.

Serves 2–4

1 small onion
1 small potato
2 handfuls of sorrel leaves
1 tbsp olive oil
350 g/12 oz broad beans, fresh or frozen
700 ml/1 ¼ pints vegetable or chicken stock
Salt and freshly milled black pepper, to taste

Cream or crème fraîche, to serve

1. Finely chop the onion. Chop the potato into small pieces. Roughly chop the sorrel leaves.
2. *Blender-style soup maker* – Put the oil into the glass jar. Set the timer to 30 minutes and the temperature to high. Add the onion, cover and cook for 1 minute using the stir button occasionally. Add the potato and broad beans, cover and cook for 5–6 minutes until steaming, using the stir button occasionally.
3. Remove the lid and add the remaining ingredients. Cover, stir to mix and bring to the boil for 3–4 minutes, then reduce the heat to simmer and cook for the remaining time using the stir button occasionally. Blend until smooth.
4. If necessary, season to taste. Ladle or pour the piping hot soup into bowls. Top with a swirl of cream or crème fraîche and serve immediately.

Jug-style soup maker
Thaw the broad beans if frozen.

Put all the prepared ingredients (step 1 above) and other ingredients into the metal jug. (The level of total ingredients must be above the minimum mark and below the maximum.) Secure the lid in place. Select the purée function and leave to cook. Season to taste, if necessary. Serve the soup as in step 4 above.

Vegetable Soup with Quinoa

Quinoa is a grain with a nutty flavour and a firm texture.

Serves 2–4

1 medium leek
2 carrots
1 garlic clove
1 piece Savoy cabbage, about 200g/7 oz
2 tbsp sunflower oil
½ tsp fennel seeds
700 ml/1 ¼ pints vegetable or chicken stock
150 g/5 ½ oz ready-to-eat quinoa
Salt and freshly milled black pepper, to taste

Hot rolls, to serve

1. Finely chop the leek, carrots and garlic. Thinly slice the cabbage.
2. *Blender-style soup maker* – Put the oil into the glass jar. Set the timer to 30 minutes and the temperature to high. Add the chopped leek, carrots, garlic and cabbage, cover and cook for 6–8 minutes until beginning to steam using the stir button occasionally. Reduce the heat if beginning to brown too much.
3. Remove the lid and add the remaining ingredients except the quinoa. Cover, stir to mix and bring to the boil for 2 minutes. Reduce the heat to simmer and cook for the remaining time using the stir button occasionally.
4. Whilst the soup is cooking, heat the quinoa following packet instructions.
5. Blend the soup to the consistency you prefer. Stir in the piping hot quinoa and blend for a second.
6. If necessary, season to taste. Ladle or pour the piping hot soup into bowls. Serve immediately with hot rolls.

Jug-style soup maker
Put all the prepared ingredients (step 1 above) and other ingredients except the quinoa into the metal jug. (The level of total ingredients must be above the minimum mark and below the maximum.) Secure the lid in place. Select the chunky function and leave to cook. Blend to the consistency you prefer. Follow steps 4 and 5 above to heat, add and blend the quinoa. Season to taste, if necessary, and serve as in step 6 above.

5

SOUP ADVENTURE

It's always nice to try something different, and included here are some soup ideas with possibly new and untried ingredients. You could find yourself hunting for nettles. Look out for the creamy chowders too, rich tasting and flavoursome, and smoked salmon is lovely in a rich velvety soup.

Nettle and Lettuce Soup

A favourite soup of mine. I like using nettles, which can usually be found, in season, growing in the garden or on nearby open ground. Wear gloves to pick the new tiny nettle leaves and carefully shake to remove any insects. Serve with warm breadsticks.

Serves 2–4

4–6 large handfuls of nettle tops or spinach leaves
½ cos lettuce
6 spring onions
1 tbsp plain flour
2 tsp lemon juice
1 tbsp olive oil
700 ml/1 ¼ pints good quality vegetable or chicken stock
Salt and freshly milled black pepper, to taste

Single cream, to serve

1. Thoroughly wash the nettle tops or spinach leaves in plenty of cold water. Chop the lettuce and thinly slice the spring onions.
2. *Blender-style soup maker* – Place everything in the glass jar and cover with the lid. Set the timer to 20 minutes and the temperature to high. Stir to mix. Bring to the boil for 2 minutes, reduce the heat to simmer and cook for the remaining time. Use the stir button occasionally. Blend until smooth.
3. If necessary, season to taste. Ladle or pour the piping hot soup into bowls. Top each bowl with a swirl of cream and serve immediately.

Jug-style soup maker
Put all the prepared ingredients (step 1 above) and other ingredients into the metal jug. (The level of total ingredients must be above the minimum mark and below the maximum.) Secure the lid in place. Select the purée function and leave to cook. If necessary, season to taste and serve immediately as in step 3 above.

Puy Lentil and Vegetable Soup

Puy lentils have a delicious flavour and are popular in France. They are available in tins or in pouches, ready-to-eat, no cooking needed.

Serves 2–4

2 small leeks
3 garlic cloves
2 medium carrots
Large handful of spinach leaves
2 tbsp olive oil
¼–½ tsp harissa paste
2 tsp ground coriander
2 tsp lemon juice

700 ml/1 ¼ pints vegetable or
   chicken stock
200 g/7 oz cooked puy lentils
150 ml/¼ pint thick Greek yogurt,
   drained
4 tbsp chopped coriander leaves
Salt and freshly milled black pepper,
   to taste

Natural yogurt and coriander leaves, to serve

1. Thinly slice the leeks, crush the garlic and roughly chop the carrots into small cubes. Tear the spinach leaves, if large, into smaller pieces.
2. *Blender-style soup maker* – Put the oil into the glass jar. Set the timer to 30 minutes and the temperature to high. Add the sliced leek and garlic, cover and cook for 3–4 minutes using the stir button occasionally until they begin to steam, but without browning too much. Add the carrots, cover, stir and cook for 3 minutes, using the stir button occasionally, until they begin to steam.
3. Add the remaining ingredients except the yogurt and chopped coriander leaves. Cover, stir to mix and bring to the boil for 2 minutes. Reduce the heat to simmer and cook for the remaining time using the stir button occasionally. Blend to the consistency you prefer. Add the yogurt and chopped coriander, cover and blend for a few seconds to mix. If necessary, season to taste.
4. Ladle or pour the piping hot soup into bowls. Top with extra yogurt and coriander leaves and serve immediately.

Jug-style soup maker
Put all the prepared ingredients (step 1 above) and other ingredients except the yogurt and chopped coriander leaves into the metal jug. (The level of total ingredients must be above the minimum mark and below the maximum.) Secure the lid in place. Select the purée function and leave to cook. Add the yogurt and chopped coriander, cover and blend for a second. Season to taste, if necessary, and serve the soup as in step 4 above.

Salmon and Sweetcorn Chowder

A mid-week soup, a good standby and very adaptable.

Serves 2–4

1 onion
1 medium potato
2 tomatoes
1 small lemon
150 g/5 ½ oz sweetcorn kernels, fresh, canned or frozen
200 g can salmon
1 tbsp olive oil
1 tsp butter
2 tsp plain flour
2 tbsp chopped parsley
400 ml/14 fl oz milk
300 ml/ ½ pint vegetable or chicken stock
Salt and freshly milled black pepper, to taste

Parsley sprigs, to serve

1. Finely chop the onion. Chop the potato into small pieces. Slice the tomatoes. Finely grate the lemon rind, cut in half and squeeze out the juice. Drain the sweetcorn – if using canned. Drain the salmon and remove any bones.
2. *Blender-style soup maker* – Put the oil and butter into the glass jar. Set the timer to 25 minutes and the temperature to high. Add the onion, cover and cook for 1–2 minutes using the stir button occasionally. Add the potato, cover and cook for 2–3 minutes using the stir button occasionally until beginning to steam.
3. Remove the lid and add the remaining ingredients except the salmon. Cover, stir to mix and bring to the boil for 2–3 minutes. Reduce the heat to simmer and cook for 15 minutes using the stir button occasionally. Add the salmon and cover and cook for the remaining time. Blend until smooth.
4. If necessary, season to taste. Ladle or pour the piping hot soup into bowls. Top with a parsley sprig and serve immediately.

Jug-style soup maker
Thaw frozen sweetcorn.

Put all the prepared ingredients (step 1 above) and other ingredients into the metal jug. (The level of total ingredients must be above the minimum mark and below the maximum.) Secure the lid in place. Select the purée function and leave to cook. Season to taste if necessary. Serve as in step 4 above.

Celeriac, Celery and Walnut Soup

Celeriac is a knobbly root vegetable and tastes like celery.

Serves 2–3

2 shallots
1 celeriac, about 500 g/1 lb 2 oz
2 celery stalks
2 tbsp olive oil
1 tbsp lime juice
1 tsp fennel seeds
700 ml/1 ¼ pints chicken or vegetable stock
Salt and freshly milled black pepper, to taste
Handful of broken walnut pieces

Walnut oil or olive oil, to drizzle, and walnut pieces, to serve

1. Finely chop the shallots. Peel the celeriac and cut into small cubes. Thinly slice the celery.
2. *Blender-style soup maker* – Put the oil into the glass jar. Set the timer to 30 minutes and the temperature to high. Add the shallots, cover and cook for 2 minutes using the stir button occasionally until they begin to steam, but without browning too much. Add the celeriac and celery, cover, stir and cook for 5 minutes, using the stir button occasionally, until they begin to steam.
3. Add the remaining ingredients except the walnut pieces. Cover, stir to mix and bring to the boil for 2–3 minutes. Reduce the heat to simmer and cook for the remaining time using the stir button occasionally. Blend to the consistency you prefer. Add the walnut pieces, cover and blend for a second to mix. If necessary, season to taste.
4. Ladle or pour the piping hot soup into bowls. Top with a drizzle of walnut oil or olive oil, sprinkle over some walnut pieces and serve immediately.

Jug-style soup maker
Put all the prepared ingredients (step 1 above) and other ingredients into the metal jug. (The level of total ingredients must be above the minimum mark and below the maximum.) Secure the lid in place. Select the purée function and leave to cook. Season to taste, if necessary, and serve the soup as in step 4 above.

Aubergine Soup with Pine Nuts

The ground spices and pine nuts give delicious flavour to this aubergine soup.

Serves 2–4

2 shallots
3 garlic cloves
2 aubergines
1 lemon
2 tbsp olive oil
2 tsp ground coriander
2 tsp ground cumin
Handful of toasted pine nuts
700 ml/1 ¼ pints chicken or vegetable stock
Salt and freshly milled black pepper, to taste

Olive oil, toasted pine nuts and lemon wedges, to serve

1. Finely chop the shallots and garlic. Trim stalks from the aubergines and cut into small cubes. Grate half of the lemon, cut in half and squeeze out the juice.
2. *Blender-style soup maker* – Put the oil into the glass jar. Set the timer to 30 minutes and the temperature to high. Add the shallots and garlic, cover and cook for 1 minute using the stir button occasionally. Remove the lid and add the aubergines. Cover and cook for 6 minutes using the stir button occasionally. Add the remaining ingredients, cover, stir to mix and bring to the boil for 2–3 minutes, then reduce the heat to simmer and cook for the remaining time using the stir button occasionally. Blend to the consistency you prefer.
3. If necessary, season to taste. Ladle or pour the piping hot soup into bowls. Drizzle over a few drops of oil and add a few pine nuts and a lemon wedge on the side. Serve immediately.

Jug-style soup maker
Put all the prepared ingredients (step 1 above) and other ingredients into the metal jug. (The level of total ingredients must be above the minimum mark and below the maximum.) Secure the lid in place. Select the purée function and leave to cook. Season to taste, if necessary, and serve the soup as in step 3 above.

Swiss Chard and Chickpea Soup

Swiss chard is a colourful leafy vegetable, rather different from spinach, but either works well.

Serves 2–4

1 onion
200 g/7 oz Swiss chard or spinach leaves
400 g can chickpeas
1 tbsp olive oil
1 tsp mixed dried herbs
850 ml/1 ½ pints vegetable or chicken stock
Salt and freshly milled black pepper, to taste

Cream or yogurt, to serve

1. Finely chop the onion. Cut the green leaves from the chard stems and thinly slice both the stems and the green part, or tear the spinach leaves. Drain the chickpeas.
2. *Blender-style soup maker* – Put the oil into the glass jar. Set the timer to 30 minutes and the temperature to high. Add the onion, cover and cook for 1–2 minutes using the stir button occasionally until beginning to steam, but without browning too much. Add the Swiss chard or spinach, cover and cook for 5 minutes using the stir button occasionally until beginning to steam.
3. Remove the lid and add the remaining ingredients. Cover, stir to mix and bring to the boil. Reduce the heat to simmer and cook for the remaining time using the stir button occasionally. Leave the soup chunky or blend to the consistency you prefer.
4. If necessary, season to taste. Ladle or pour the piping hot soup into bowls. Swirl over a little cream or yogurt and serve immediately.

Jug-style soup maker
Put all the prepared ingredients (step 1 above) and other ingredients into the metal jug. (The level of total ingredients must be above the minimum mark and below the maximum.) Secure the lid in place. Select the chunky function and leave to cook. Season to taste, if necessary, and blend to the consistency you prefer. Serve as in step 4 above.

Red Pepper Soup with Smoked Salmon

The salmon at the bottom of the bowl warms through nicely in the soup.

Serves 2–4

3 red peppers
Small bunch of dill
200 g/7 oz smoked salmon slices or pieces
1 tbsp olive oil
200 g can chopped tomatoes
1 tbsp lime juice
700 ml/1 ¼ pints chicken or vegetable stock
Salt and freshly milled black pepper, to taste

Soured cream, salmon caviar and dill leaves, to serve

1. Cut the red peppers in half, remove the stalks and seeds and dice. Finely chop the dill. Thinly slice the smoked salmon pieces.
2. *Blender-style soup maker* – Put the oil into the glass jar. Set the timer to 20 minutes and the temperature to high. Add the red pepper slices, cover and cook for 5–6 minutes until steaming, using the stir button occasionally.
3. Remove the lid and add the remaining ingredients except the smoked salmon. Cover, stir to mix and bring to the boil, then reduce the heat to simmer and cook for the remaining time using the stir button occasionally.
4. Blend the soup to the consistency you prefer. If necessary, season to taste.
5. Arrange the salmon strips in the base of the soup bowls. Ladle or spoon the piping hot soup over the fish. Top each bowl with a blob of soured cream, some salmon caviar and dill leaves. Serve immediately.

Jug-style soup maker
Put all the prepared ingredients except the smoked salmon (step 1 above) and the other ingredients into the metal jug. (The level of total ingredients must be above the minimum mark and below the maximum.) Secure the lid in place. Select the purée function and leave to cook. Season to taste if necessary. Serve the soup as in step 5 above.

Beetroot, Tomato and Rosemary Soup

Fabulous colour and depth of flavour.

Serves 2–4

1 large red onion
1 small potato
5 cooked beetroots
1 small sprig of fresh rosemary
2 tbsp sunflower oil
400 g can tomatoes
¼ tsp sugar
700 ml/1 ¼ pints chicken or vegetable stock
150 ml/¼ pint crème fraîche or Greek yogurt
Salt and freshly milled black pepper, to taste

Crème fraîche or Greek yogurt, to serve

1. Finely chop the onion and cut the potato and beetroots into small cubes. Pull the rosemary leaves from the stalk and finely chop.
2. *Blender-style soup maker* – Put the oil into the glass jar. Set the timer to 30 minutes and the temperature to high. Add the onion, cover and cook for 1 minute using the stir button occasionally. Remove the lid and add the remaining ingredients except the crème fraîche or yogurt. Cover, stir to mix and bring to the boil for 2–3 minutes, then reduce the heat to simmer and cook for the remaining time using the stir button occasionally. Blend to the consistency you prefer. Add the crème fraîche or yogurt, cover and blend for a second.
3. If necessary, season to taste. Ladle or pour the piping hot soup into bowls, top with a swirl of crème fraîche or yogurt and serve immediately.

Jug-style soup maker
Put all the prepared ingredients (step 1 above) and other ingredients except the crème fraîche or yogurt into the metal jug. (The level of total ingredients must be above the minimum mark and below the maximum.) Secure the lid in place. Select the purée function and leave to cook. Add the crème fraîche or yogurt, replace the lid and blend for a second. Season to taste, if necessary, and serve the soup as in step 3 above.

Turkey and Sweetcorn Chowder

A New World dish.

Serves 2–4

1 onion
1 celery stick
1 medium potato
150 g/5 ½ oz sweetcorn kernels, fresh, canned or frozen
140 g/5 oz turkey breast meat
1 tbsp olive oil
1 tsp butter
2 tbsp chopped fennel leaves
400 ml/14 fl oz milk
300 ml/ ½ pint turkey or chicken stock
2 tbsp cream or yogurt
Salt and freshly milled black pepper, to taste

Fennel leaves, to serve

1. Finely chop the onion. Thinly slice the celery stick. Chop the potato into small pieces. Drain the sweetcorn – if using canned. Cut the turkey meat into small pieces.
2. *Blender-style soup maker* – Put the oil and butter into the glass jar. Set the timer to 30 minutes and the temperature to high. Add the turkey, cover and cook for 3–4 minutes until the turkey is cooked through using the stir button occasionally. Add the onion and celery, cover and cook for 2–3 minutes using the stir button occasionally until beginning to steam.
3. Remove the lid and add the remaining ingredients except the cream or yogurt. Cover, stir to mix and bring to the boil for 2–3 minutes. Reduce the heat to simmer and cook for the remaining time using the stir button occasionally. Blend until smooth. Add the cream or yogurt, cover and blend for a second.
4. If necessary, season to taste. Ladle or pour the piping hot soup into bowls. Top with a fennel leaf and serve immediately.

Jug-style soup maker
Thaw frozen sweetcorn. Use cooked turkey meat not raw.

Put all the prepared ingredients (step 1 above) and other ingredients except the cream and yogurt into the metal jug. (The level of total ingredients must be above the minimum mark and below the maximum.) Secure the lid in place. Select the purée function and leave to cook. Add the cream or yogurt, cover and blend for a second. Season to taste if necessary. Serve as in step 4 above.

Prawn and Saffron Soup

Golden strands of saffron – a little goes a long way.

Serves 2–4

1 bunch of spring onions
4 ripe tomatoes
Small bunch of tarragon
1 tbsp olive oil
Pinch of saffron strands
2 tbsp ground almonds
1 tbsp lemon juice
2 tbsp fish sauce
3 tbsp dry white wine or vodka (optional)
700 ml/1 ¼ pints vegetable or chicken stock
280 g/10 oz cooked peeled prawns
Salt and freshly milled black pepper, to taste

Toasted almonds and tarragon leaves, to serve

1. Thinly slice the spring onions. Chop the tomatoes. Pull the tarragon leaves from the stalks and finely chop.
2. *Blender-style soup maker* – Put the oil into the glass jar. Set the timer to 20 minutes and the temperature to high. Add the spring onions, cover and cook for 2–3 minutes until steaming, using the stir button occasionally.
3. Remove the lid and add the remaining ingredients except the prawns. Cover, stir to mix and bring to the boil, then reduce the heat to simmer and cook for 10 minutes using the stir button occasionally. Add the prawns and cook for the remaining time using the stir button occasionally. Blend to the consistency you prefer.
4. If necessary, season to taste. Ladle or spoon the piping hot soup into bowls. Top with toasted almonds and tarragon leaves and serve immediately.

Jug-style soup maker
Put all the prepared ingredients (step 1 above) and the other ingredients into the metal jug. (The level of total ingredients must be above the minimum mark and below the maximum.) Secure the lid in place. Select the purée function and leave to cook. Season to taste if necessary. Serve the soup as in step 4 above.

Oriental Chicken and Noodle Soup

Hints of the Orient.

Serves 2–4

1 bunch of spring onions
1 celery stick
90 g/3 ¼ oz mushrooms
2 big handfuls of pak choi leaves
300 g/10 ½ oz boneless fresh
   chicken
1 tbsp olive oil
1 tsp garlic purée

1 tsp ginger purée
1 tbsp light soy sauce
700 ml/1 ¼ pints chicken stock
300 g packet of ready-cooked egg
   noodles
Salt and freshly milled black pepper,
   to taste

Prawn crackers, to serve

1. Thinly slice the spring onions. Thinly slice the celery stick. Roughly chop the mushrooms. Finely slice the pak choi leaves. Cut the chicken into small pieces.
2. *Blender-style soup maker* – Put the oil into the glass jar. Set the timer to 30 minutes and the temperature to simmer. Add the chicken, spring onions and celery, cover and cook for 15–18 minutes until the chicken is cooked through using the stir button occasionally. Increase the heat to high.
3. Remove the lid and add the remaining ingredients except the noodles. Cover, stir to mix and bring to the boil for 2 minutes. Reduce the heat to simmer and cook for the remaining time using the stir button occasionally.
4. Whilst the soup is cooking, cook the noodles following the packet instructions.
5. Blend to the consistency you prefer. If necessary, season to taste. Heap the piping hot noodles in soup bowls. Ladle or pour the piping hot soup over. Serve immediately with prawn crackers.

Jug-style soup maker
Use cooked chicken, not raw.

To cook the noodles follow step 4 above.

Put all the prepared ingredients (step 1 above) and other ingredients except the noodles into the metal jug. (The level of total ingredients must be above the minimum mark and below the maximum.) Secure the lid in place. Select the chunky function and leave to cook. Blend to the consistency you prefer. Season to taste if necessary. Serve as in step 5 above.

Hot Cucumber Broth with Hot Smoked Trout

Hot smoked trout is cooked and ready to use.

Serves 2–4

1 bunch of spring onions
2 cucumbers
2 courgettes
1 red chilli (see page 17)
Small bunch of dill
2–3 hot smoked trout fillets
1 tbsp olive oil
1 tbsp lemon juice
700 ml/1 ¼ pints vegetable or fish stock
Salt and freshly milled black pepper, to taste

Dill leaves and lemon wedges, to serve

1. Thinly slice the spring onions. Cut the cucumbers in half lengthways and scoop out the seeds. Chop the courgettes. Cut the chilli in half, remove the stalk and seeds and thinly slice. Finely chop the dill. Break the hot smoked trout fillets into bite-sized pieces, removing any bones.
2. *Blender-style soup maker* – Put the oil into the glass jar. Set the timer to 20 minutes and the temperature to high. Add the spring onions, cover and cook for 2–3 minutes until steaming, using the stir button occasionally.
3. Remove the lid and add the remaining ingredients except the hot smoked trout. Cover, stir to mix and bring to the boil, then reduce the heat to simmer and cook for the remaining time using the stir button occasionally.
4. Blend the soup until smooth. If necessary, season to taste. Arrange the trout pieces in the base of the soup bowls. Ladle or spoon the piping hot soup over the fish. Top with dill leaves. Serve immediately with lemon wedges on the side.

Jug-style soup maker
Put all the prepared ingredients except the hot smoked trout (step 1 above) and the other ingredients into the metal jug. (The level of total ingredients must be above the minimum mark and below the maximum.) Secure the lid in place. Select the purée function and leave to cook. Season to taste if necessary. Serve the soup as in step 4 above.

Prawn and Saffron Soup with Noodles

For surf and turf, add in some chicken.

Serves 2–4

1 bunch of spring onions
½ small Chinese lettuce
1 tbsp olive oil
Pinch of saffron strands
1 tbsp lemon juice
2 tbsp fish sauce
700 ml/1 ¼ pints chicken stock
280 g/10 oz cooked peeled prawns
300 g packet of ready-cooked egg noodles
Salt and freshly milled black pepper, to taste

Prawn crackers, to serve

1. Thinly slice the spring onions. Finely slice the Chinese lettuce.
2. *Blender-style soup maker* – Put the oil into the glass jar. Set the timer to 20 minutes and the temperature to high. Add the spring onions, cover and cook for 2–3 minutes until steaming, using the stir button occasionally. Remove the lid and add the remaining ingredients except the prawns and noodles. Cover, stir to mix and bring to the boil, then reduce the heat to simmer and cook for 10 minutes using the stir button occasionally.
3. Add the prawns and cook for the remaining time using the stir button occasionally.
4. Whilst the soup is cooking, cook the noodles following the packet instructions.
5. Blend the soup to the consistency you prefer. If necessary, season to taste. Heap the piping hot noodles into soup bowls. Ladle or pour the piping hot soup over. Serve immediately with prawn crackers.

Jug-style soup maker
To cook the noodles follow step 4 above

Put all the prepared ingredients (step 1 above) and other ingredients except the noodles into the metal jug. (The level of total ingredients must be above the minimum mark and below the maximum.) Secure the lid in place. Select the chunky function and leave to cook. Blend to the consistency you prefer. Season to taste if necessary. Serve as in step 5 above.

Turkey Soup with Rice Noodles

Lots of flavours happening here.

Serves 2–4

4 spring onions	1 tbsp olive oil
1 small leek	2 tsp chilli paste
1 carrot	1 tbsp fish sauce
2 garlic cloves	700 ml/1 ¼ pints chicken stock
About ¼ of a Savoy cabbage	300 g packet of fresh rice noodles
2.5 cm/1 inch piece of fresh root ginger	Salt and freshly milled black pepper, to taste
300 g/10 ½ oz boneless fresh turkey	

1. Thinly slice the spring onions, leek and carrot and crush the garlic. Finely slice the Savoy cabbage. Grate the ginger. Cut the turkey into small pieces.
2. *Blender-style soup maker* – Put the oil into the glass jar. Set the timer to 30 minutes and the temperature to simmer. Add the turkey, spring onions and leek, cover and cook for 15–18 minutes until the turkey is cooked through using the stir button occasionally. Increase the heat to high.
3. Remove the lid and add the remaining ingredients except the rice noodles. Cover, stir to mix and bring to the boil for 2 minutes. Reduce the heat to simmer and cook for the remaining time using the stir button occasionally.
4. Whilst the soup is cooking, cook the rice noodles following the packet instructions.
5. Blend the soup to the consistency you prefer. If necessary, season to taste. Heap the piping hot rice noodles into soup bowls. Ladle or pour the piping hot soup over. Serve immediately.

Jug-style soup maker
Use cooked turkey, not raw.

To cook the rice noodles follow step 4 above.

Put all the prepared ingredients (step 1 above) and other ingredients except the noodles into the metal jug. (The level of total ingredients must be above the minimum mark and below the maximum.) Secure the lid in place. Select the chunky function and leave to cook. Blend to the consistency you prefer. Season to taste if necessary. Serve with the noodles as in step 5 above.

Corn and Red Onion Soup

A rich and earthy soup.

Serves 2–4

350 g/12 oz red onions
2 tbsp cornflour
700 ml/1 ¼ pints beef stock
2 tbsp sunflower oil
200 g/7 oz sweetcorn
1 tsp beef extract
Salt and freshly milled black pepper, to taste

Grated hard cheese, to serve

1. Thinly slice the onions. Put the cornflour into a small cup and stir in 2–3 tbsp of the stock until blended.
2. *Blender-style soup maker* – Put the oil into the glass jar. Set the timer to 30 minutes and the temperature to high. Add the onion, cover and cook for 6–8 minutes using the stir button occasionally. Remove the lid and add the remaining ingredients. Cover, stir to mix and bring to the boil for 2–3 minutes, then reduce the heat to simmer and cook for the remaining time using the stir button occasionally.
3. If necessary, season to taste. Ladle or pour the piping hot soup into bowls. Top with a little grated cheese. Serve immediately.

Jug-style soup maker
Put all the prepared ingredients (step 1 above) and other ingredients into the metal jug. (The level of total ingredients must be above the minimum mark and below the maximum.) Secure the lid in place. Select the chunky function and leave to cook. Season to taste if necessary, and serve the soup as in step 3 above.

6

SOUP MISCELLANY

A final sampling of savoury and delicious soups, smooth or chunky as usual, to round off the hot soup sequence. More creamy chowders and another good mix of vegetables are to be found here. Be sure to seek out and buy the best quality vegetables and other ingredients for your soups – good quality always shows through in the taste.

Courgette, Leek and Tomato Rice Soup

A soup with the flavours of risotto.

Serves 2–4

1 medium leek
2 courgettes
1 garlic clove
1 red chilli (see page 17)
2–3 sprigs of oregano
2 tbsp sunflower oil
400 g can tomatoes
425 ml/¾ pint vegetable or chicken stock
4 heaped tbsp cooked white or brown rice
Salt and freshly milled black pepper, to taste

Pecorino or Parmesan shavings, to serve

1. Finely chop the leek, courgettes and garlic. Cut the chilli in half, remove and discard the seeds and finely chop. Pull the oregano leaves from the stalks.
2. *Blender-style soup maker* – Put the oil into the glass jar. Set the timer to 30 minutes and the temperature to high. Add the chopped leek, cover and cook for 2 minutes using the stir button occasionally.
3. Remove the lid and add the remaining ingredients except the rice. Cover, stir to mix, and bring to the boil for 2 minutes. Reduce the heat to simmer and cook for 20 minutes using the stir button occasionally. Add the cooked rice and cook for the remaining time.
4. If necessary, season to taste. Ladle or pour the piping hot soup into bowls. Scatter over a few Pecorino or Parmesan shavings and serve immediately.

Jug-style soup maker
Use piping hot rice.

Put all the prepared ingredients (step 1 above) and other ingredients, except the rice, into the metal jug. (The level of total ingredients must be above the minimum mark and below the maximum.) Secure the lid in place. Select the chunky function and leave to cook. Stir in the piping hot rice, season to taste, if necessary and serve as in step 4 above.

Cheesy Potato, Spring Onion and Pesto Soup

Jars of spices and pastes give instant flavour to simple dishes.

Serves 2–4

1 bunch of spring onions
2 medium potatoes
1 tbsp olive oil
1 tbsp butter
700 ml/1 ¼ pints vegetable or chicken stock
150 ml/ ¼ pint milk
4 tbsp green or red pesto
60 g/2 ¼ oz grated hard cheese
Salt and freshly milled black pepper, to taste

Croûtons, to serve

1. Thinly slice the spring onions. Finely chop the potatoes.
2. *Blender-style soup maker* – Put the oil and butter into the glass jar. Set the timer to 30 minutes and the temperature to high. Add the spring onions, cover and cook for 1 minute using the stir button occasionally. Add the potatoes, cover and cook for 3–4 minutes until steaming, using the stir button occasionally.
3. Remove the lid and add the remaining ingredients except the grated cheese. Cover, stir to mix and bring to the boil for 2–3 minutes, then reduce the heat to simmer and cook for the remaining time using the stir button occasionally. Blend until smooth. Add the cheese, cover and blend for a second.
4. If necessary, season to taste. Ladle or pour the piping hot soup into bowls and top with a few croûtons. Serve immediately.

Jug-style soup maker
Put all the prepared ingredients (step 1 above) and other ingredients, except the cheese, into the metal jug. (The level of total ingredients must be above the minimum mark and below the maximum.) Secure the lid in place. Select the purée function and leave to cook. Add the cheese, cover and blend for a second. Season to taste if necessary. Serve the soup as in step 4 above.

French Onion Soup

My version of a classic for the soup maker.

Serves 2–4

650 g/1 lb 7 oz onions
1 garlic clove
2 tbsp cornflour
700 ml/1 ¼ pints beef stock
2 tbsp sunflower oil
1 tsp beef extract
Salt and freshly milled black pepper, to taste

Cheese floats (see page 123) or grated hard cheese, to serve

1. Thinly slice the onions and crush the garlic. Put the cornflour into a small cup and stir in 2–3 tbsp of the stock until blended.
2. *Blender-style soup maker* – Put the oil into the glass jar. Set the timer to 30 minutes and the temperature to high. Add the onion and garlic, cover and cook for 6–8 minutes using the stir button occasionally. Remove the lid and add the remaining ingredients. Cover, stir to mix and bring to the boil for 2–3 minutes, then reduce the heat to simmer and cook for the remaining time using the stir button occasionally.
3. If necessary, season to taste. Ladle or pour the piping hot soup into bowls. Top with a cheese float or grated cheese. Serve immediately.

Jug-style soup maker
Put all the prepared ingredients (step 1 above) and other ingredients into the metal jug. (The level of total ingredients must be above the minimum mark and below the maximum.) Secure the lid in place. Select the chunky function and leave to cook. Season to taste, if necessary, and serve the soup as in step 3 above.

Roasted Vegetable Soup

Here's a great idea for using that packet of frozen mixed vegetables.

Serves 2–4

500 g packet frozen roasted vegetables
6 tomatoes
700 ml/1 ¼ pints chicken or vegetable stock
1 tsp dried mixed herbs
3 tbsp tomato ketchup
Salt and freshly milled black pepper, to taste

Crusty bread, to serve

1. If too large, cut the roasted vegetables into smaller pieces. Chop the tomatoes.
2. *Blender-style soup maker* – Set the timer to 20 minutes and the temperature to high. Add all the ingredients, cover, stir and bring to the boil for 2–3 minutes, then reduce the heat to simmer and cook for the remaining time using the stir button occasionally. Leave chunky or blend as you prefer.
3. If necessary, season to taste. Ladle or spoon the piping hot soup into bowls and serve immediately.

Jug-style soup maker
Thaw the vegetables if frozen and, if too large, cut into smaller pieces.

Put all the prepared ingredients (step 1 above) and other ingredients into the metal jug. (The level of total ingredients must be above the minimum mark and below the maximum.) Secure the lid in place. Select the chunky function and leave to cook. Leave chunky or blend as you prefer. Season to taste if necessary. Serve the soup as in step 3 above.

Corn Chowder

A smooth sweetcorn soup with aromatic thyme leaves.

Serves 2–4

1 onion
2 celery sticks
1 medium potato
280 g/10 oz sweetcorn kernels, fresh, canned or frozen
1 tbsp olive oil
1 tsp butter
A few thyme leaves
400 ml/14 fl oz milk
300 ml/½ pint vegetable or chicken stock
Salt and freshly milled black pepper, to taste

Thyme leaves, to serve

1. Finely chop the onion. Thinly slice the celery sticks. Chop the potato into small pieces. Drain the sweetcorn – if using canned.
2. *Blender-style soup maker* – Put the oil and butter into the glass jar. Set the timer to 30 minutes and the temperature to high. Add the onion, cover and cook for 1–2 minutes using the stir button occasionally until beginning to steam. Add the celery, cover and cook for 5–6 minutes using the stir button occasionally until beginning to steam.
3. Remove the lid and add the remaining ingredients. Cover, stir to mix and bring to the boil for 2 minutes. Reduce the heat to simmer and cook for the remaining time using the stir button occasionally. Blend until still smooth.
4. If necessary, season to taste. Ladle or pour the piping hot soup into bowls. Top with a few thyme leaves and serve immediately.

Jug-style soup maker
Thaw frozen sweetcorn.
   Put all the prepared ingredients (step 1 above) and other ingredients into the metal jug. (The level of total ingredients must be above the minimum mark and below the maximum.) Secure the lid in place. Select the purée function and leave to cook. Season to taste if necessary. Serve as in step 4 above.

Pea and Sweetcorn Chowder

Delicious with hot garlic bread.

Serves 2–4

1 medium potato
150 g/5½ oz sweetcorn kernels, fresh, canned or frozen
1 tbsp olive oil
150 g/5½ oz peas, fresh or frozen
2 tsp plain flour
400 ml/14 fl oz milk
300 ml/½ pint chicken or vegetable stock
1 tsp mint sauce
Salt and freshly milled black pepper, to taste

Hot garlic bread, to serve

1. Chop the potato into small pieces. Drain the sweetcorn – if using canned.
2. *Blender-style soup maker* – Put the oil into the glass jar. Set the timer to 25 minutes and the temperature to high. Add the potato, cover and cook for 1–2 minutes using the stir button occasionally until it begins to steam. Remove the lid and add the remaining ingredients. Cover, stir to mix and bring to the boil for 2–3 minutes. Reduce the heat to simmer and cook for the remaining time. Blend until smooth.
3. If necessary, season to taste. Ladle or pour the piping hot soup into bowls. Serve immediately with hot garlic bread on the side.

Jug-style soup maker
Thaw frozen sweetcorn and peas.

Put all the prepared ingredients (step 1 above) and other ingredients into the metal jug. (The level of total ingredients must be above the minimum mark and below the maximum.) Secure the lid in place. Select the purée function and leave to cook. Season to taste if necessary. Serve as in step 3 above.

Savoy Cabbage and Parsnip Soup

Savoy cabbage, with its crimped and curly leaves, has a mild flavour which won't overpower the parsnip.

Serves 2–4

1 medium red onion
2 medium parsnips
Slice of savoy cabbage, about 200 g/7 oz
1 tbsp sunflower oil
700 ml/1 ¼ pints chicken or vegetable stock
Salt and freshly milled black pepper, to taste

Hot bacon pieces, to serve (optional)

1. Finely chop the onion. Roughly chop the parsnips into small pieces. Thinly slice the cabbage.
2. *Blender-style soup maker* – Put the oil into the glass jar. Set the timer to 30 minutes and the temperature to high. Add the onion, cover and cook for 1–2 minutes using the stir button occasionally until it begins to steam. Add the parsnips and cabbage. Cover, stir and cook for 5–6 minutes using the stir button occasionally until beginning to steam.
3. Add the remaining ingredients. Cover, stir to mix and bring to the boil for 2 minutes. Reduce the heat to simmer and cook for the remaining time using the stir button occasionally. Blend to the consistency you prefer. If necessary, season to taste.
4. Ladle or pour the piping hot soup into bowls. Top with a few hot bacon pieces, if using, and serve immediately.

Jug-style soup maker
Put all the prepared ingredients (step 1 above) and other ingredients into the metal jug. (The level of total ingredients must be above the minimum mark and below the maximum.) Secure the lid in place. Select the purée function and leave to cook. Season to taste, if necessary, and serve the soup as in step 4 above.

Lemon Chicken and Mushroom Soup

A great pick-me-up, and very refreshing.

Serves 2–4

2 shallots
2 celery sticks
150 g/5 ½ oz mushrooms
300 g/10 ½ oz boneless fresh chicken
1 lemon
1 tbsp olive oil
2 handfuls of small spinach leaves
700 ml/1 ¼ pints chicken stock
Salt and freshly milled black pepper, to taste

Lemon wedges and crusty bread, to serve

1. Finely chop the shallots. Thinly slice the celery sticks. Roughly chop the mushrooms. Cut the chicken into small pieces. Grate the rind from the lemon, cut in half and squeeze out the juice.
2. *Blender-style soup maker* – Put the oil into the glass jar. Set the timer to 30 minutes and the temperature to simmer. Add the chicken, shallots and celery, cover and cook for 15–18 minutes until the chicken is cooked through using the stir button occasionally. Increase the heat to high.
3. Remove the lid and add the remaining ingredients. Cover, stir to mix and bring to the boil for 2 minutes. Reduce the heat to simmer and cook for the remaining time using the stir button occasionally. Blend until smooth.
4. If necessary, season to taste. Ladle or pour the piping hot soup into bowls. Serve immediately with lemon wedges and crusty bread.

Jug-style soup maker
Use cooked chicken, not raw.

Put all the prepared ingredients (step 1 above) and other ingredients into the metal jug. (The level of total ingredients must be above the minimum mark and below the maximum.) Secure the lid in place. Select the chunky function and leave to cook. Blend to the consistency you prefer. Season to taste if necessary. Serve as in step 4 above.

Fennel Soup

Fennel packs a punch with its wonderful aniseed flavour.

Serves 2–4

1 large onion
2 garlic cloves
2 fennel bulbs about 280 g/10 oz
1 tbsp olive oil
700 ml/1 ¼ pints vegetable or chicken stock
Salt and freshly milled white pepper, to taste

Cream or crème fraîche and fennel leaves, to serve

1. Finely chop the onion and crush the garlic. Cut the fronds from the fennel and reserve some for a garnish. Finely chop the remaining fronds and the fennel bulbs.
2. *Blender-style soup maker* – Put the oil into the glass jar. Set the timer to 30 minutes and the temperature to high. Add the onion and garlic, cover and cook for 1 minute using the stir button occasionally. Add the fennel, cover and cook for 6–8 minutes until steaming, using the stir button occasionally.
3. Remove the lid and add the remaining ingredients. Cover, stir to mix and bring to the boil for 3–4 minutes, then reduce the heat to simmer and cook for the remaining time using the stir button occasionally. Blend until smooth.
4. If necessary, season to taste. Ladle or pour the piping hot soup into bowls. Top with a swirl of cream or crème fraîche and fennel leaves. Serve immediately.

Jug-style soup maker
Put all the prepared ingredients (step 1 above) and other ingredients into the metal jug, reserving some fennel leaves for garnish. (The level of total ingredients must be above the minimum mark and below the maximum.) Secure the lid in place. Select the purée function and leave to cook. Blend to the consistency you prefer and season to taste, if necessary. Serve the soup as in step 4 above.

Sea-Fish Soup

A very fishy soup – choose the seafood you like.

Serves 2–4

1 medium onion
2 garlic cloves
1 carrot
200g/7 oz cooked smoked or unsmoked white fish
1 tbsp olive oil
400 g can tomatoes
2 tbsp tomato purée
1 tsp dried mixed herbs
1 tbsp lemon juice
2 tbsp fish sauce
700 ml/1 ¼ pints vegetable or chicken stock
100 g/3 ½ oz cooked peeled prawns
Salt and freshly milled black pepper, to taste

Crusty bread, to serve

1. Finely chop the onion and crush the garlic. Cut the carrot into small pieces. Skin and flake the fish, removing any bones.
2. *Blender-style soup maker* – Put the oil into the glass jar. Set the timer to 25 minutes and the temperature to high. Add the onion and garlic, cover and cook for 2–3 minutes until steaming, using the stir button occasionally.
3. Remove the lid and add the remaining ingredients except the prawns and flaked fish. Cover, stir to mix and bring to the boil, then reduce the heat to simmer and cook for 10 minutes using the stir button occasionally. Add the prawns and flaked fish and cook for the remaining time using the stir button occasionally. Blend to the consistency you prefer.
4. If necessary, season to taste. Ladle or spoon the piping hot soup into bowls. Serve immediately with crusty bread.

Jug-style soup maker
Put all the prepared ingredients (step 1 above) and the other ingredients into the metal jug. (The level of total ingredients must be above the minimum mark and below the maximum.) Secure the lid in place. Select the purée function and leave to cook. Season to taste if necessary. Serve the soup as in step 4 above.

Minestrone Soup

A soup that's also a main meal.

Serves 2–4

1 medium onion	700 ml/1 ¼ pints vegetable or
1 garlic clove	chicken stock
2 carrots	400 g can tomatoes
2 celery sticks	100 g/3 ½ oz peas
1 small potato	1 tsp dried mixed herbs
200 g can chickpeas	150 g/5 ½ oz fresh spaghetti
1 tbsp olive oil	Salt and freshly milled black pepper,
	to taste

Grated Parmesan cheese, to serve

1. Finely chop the onion and garlic. Cut the carrots into small pieces and thinly slice the celery. Finely chop the potato. Drain the chickpeas.
2. *Blender-style soup maker* – Put the oil into the glass jar. Set the timer to 30 minutes and the temperature to high. Add the onion and garlic, cover and cook for 1 minute using the stir button occasionally. Add the potato, carrots and celery, cover and cook for 5–6 minutes until steaming, using the stir button occasionally.
3. Remove the lid and add the remaining ingredients except the spaghetti. Cover, stir to mix and bring to the boil for 3–4 minutes, then reduce the heat to simmer and cook for the remaining time using the stir button occasionally.
4. Cut the spaghetti into short lengths and cook according to packet instructions.
5. Blend the soup to the consistency you prefer.
6. If necessary, season to taste. Spoon the piping hot spaghetti into soup bowls and ladle or pour the piping hot soup over. Top with Parmesan cheese and serve immediately.

Jug-style soup maker
Thaw peas, if frozen.

Put all the prepared ingredients (step 1 above) and other ingredients except the spaghetti into the metal jug. (The level of total ingredients must be above the minimum mark and below the maximum.) Secure the lid in place. Select the chunky function and leave to cook.

Cook the spaghetti (step 4 above). Blend the soup to the consistency you prefer. Season to taste if necessary. Serve the soup with piping hot spaghetti as in step 6 above.

Leek and Shallot Soup

A variation on French onion soup, but with a leek.

Serves 2–4

6 shallots
1 leek
1 potato
1 tbsp cornflour
700 ml/1 ¼ pints beef stock
2 tbsp sunflower oil
1 tsp beef extract
Salt and freshly milled black pepper, to taste

Grated hard cheese, to serve

1. Thinly slice the shallots and leek. Chop the potato into small pieces. Put the cornflour into a small cup and stir in 2–3 tbsp of the stock until blended.
2. *Blender-style soup maker* – Put the oil into the glass jar. Set the timer to 30 minutes and the temperature to high. Add the shallots and leek, cover and cook for 6–8 minutes using the stir button occasionally. Remove the lid and add the remaining ingredients. Cover, stir to mix and bring to the boil for 2–3 minutes. Reduce the heat to simmer and cook for the remaining time using the stir button occasionally. Blend until smooth.
3. If necessary, season to taste. Ladle or pour the piping hot soup into bowls. Top with a little cheese and serve immediately.

Jug-style soup maker
Put all the prepared ingredients (step 1 above) and other ingredients into the metal jug. (The level of total ingredients must be above the minimum mark and below the maximum.) Secure the lid in place. Select the purée function and leave to cook. Season to taste, if necessary, and serve the soup as in step 3 above.

Beans and Frankfurter Soup

Sure to be a family favourite.

Serves 2–4

2 medium red onions
400 g can mixed beans
1 large handful of spinach leaves
6 Frankfurter sausages
1 tbsp sunflower oil
700 ml/1 ¼ pints vegetable or chicken stock
400 g can tomatoes with herbs
1 tbsp wholegrain mustard
1 tsp dried mixed herbs
Salt and freshly milled black pepper, to taste

Hot garlic bread, to serve

1. Finely chop the onions. Drain the mixed beans. Thinly slice the spinach leaves. Thickly slice the sausages.
2. *Blender-style soup maker* – Put the oil into the glass jar. Set the timer to 30 minutes and the temperature to high. Add the onion, cover and cook for 1 minute using the stir button occasionally. Remove the lid and add the remaining ingredients except the sausages. Cover, stir to mix and bring to the boil for 5–6 minutes, then reduce the heat to simmer and cook for the remaining time using the stir button occasionally.
3. Grill or fry the sausage slices until cooked through and piping hot.
4. Blend the soup to the consistency you prefer.
5. If necessary, season to taste. Ladle or pour the piping hot soup into bowls and stir in the hot sausage slices. Serve immediately with hot garlic bread.

Jug-style soup maker
Use piping hot cooked Frankfurter sausages.

Put all the prepared ingredients except the sausage slices (step 1 above) and other ingredients, into the metal jug. (The level of total ingredients must be above the minimum mark and below the maximum.) Secure the lid in place. Select the chunky function and leave to cook. Blend the soup to the consistency you prefer. Season to taste if necessary. Serve the soup with the sausage slices as in step 5 above.

Celery, Spring Onion and Feta Soup

Feta is a simple Greek cheese. It helps to make this soup light and refreshing.

Serves 2–4

1 bunch of spring onions
1 small celery head
70 g/2 ½ oz feta cheese
1 tbsp olive oil
1 tbsp lemon juice
700 ml/1 ¼ pints vegetable or chicken stock
Salt and freshly milled white pepper, to taste

Sourdough bread, to serve

1. Thinly slice the spring onions and celery. Crumble the feta cheese onto a plate.
2. *Blender-style soup maker* – Put the oil into the glass jar. Set the timer to 30 minutes and the temperature to high. Add the spring onion and celery, cover and cook for 6–8 minutes until steaming, using the stir button occasionally
3. Remove the lid and add the remaining ingredients except the feta cheese. Cover, stir to mix and bring to the boil for 3–4 minutes, then reduce the heat to simmer and cook for the remaining time using the stir button occasionally. Blend until smooth.
4. If necessary, season to taste. Ladle or pour the piping hot soup into bowls. Top with crumbled feta cheese. Serve immediately with sourdough bread.

Jug-style soup maker
Put all the prepared ingredients except the feta cheese (step 1 above) and other ingredients into the metal jug. (The level of total ingredients must be above the minimum mark and below the maximum.) Secure the lid in place. Select the purée function and leave to cook. Season to taste if necessary. Serve the soup as in step 4 above.

Chicken and Noodle Soup

Tasty noodles lit up by soy sauce and ginger.

Serves 2–4

4 spring onions
2 garlic cloves
1 small red pepper
90 g/3 ¼ oz chestnut mushrooms
2 handfuls of pak choi leaves
2.5 cm/1 inch piece of fresh root
  ginger

300 g/10 ½ oz boneless fresh chicken
1 tbsp olive oil
2 tbsp light soy sauce
700 ml/1 ¼ pints chicken stock
300 g packet of fresh egg noodles
Salt and freshly milled black pepper,
  to taste

Prawn crackers, to serve

1. Thinly slice the spring onions and crush the garlic. Cut the pepper in half, remove the stalk and seeds and thinly slice. Roughly chop the mushrooms. Finely slice the pak choi leaves. Grate the ginger. Cut the chicken into small pieces.
2. *Blender-style soup maker* – Put the oil into the glass jar. Set the timer to 30 minutes and the temperature to simmer. Add the chicken, spring onions and celery, cover and cook for 15–18 minutes until the chicken is cooked through using the stir button occasionally. Increase the heat to high.
3. Remove the lid and add the remaining ingredients except the noodles. Cover, stir to mix and bring to the boil for 2 minutes. Reduce the heat to simmer and cook for the remaining time using the stir button occasionally.
4. Whilst the soup is cooking, cook the noodles following the packet instructions.
5. Blend to the consistency you prefer. If necessary, season to taste. Heap the piping hot noodles into soup bowls. Ladle or pour the piping hot soup over. Serve immediately with prawn crackers.

Jug-style soup maker
Use cooked chicken, not raw.
    To cook the noodles follow step 4 above
    Put all the prepared ingredients (step 1 above) and other ingredients except the noodles into the metal jug. (The level of total ingredients must be above the minimum mark and below the maximum.) Secure the lid in place. Select the chunky function and leave to cook. Blend to the consistency you prefer. Season to taste if necessary. Serve with the noodles as in step 5 above.

7

FRUITY SOUPS

Fruit soups are popular in Scandinavia and parts of eastern Europe. Elsewhere they await discovery. And they are well worth discovering, with their vibrant, refreshing flavours, sweet, sharp or tangy. They can be served as breakfast, as a mouth-watering snack or, crossing boundaries, as a dessert course soup. So they are really adaptable too.

The fruit used can be fresh or frozen, and there is a great opportunity here to make the most of a glut of garden fruits or hedgerow fruits, such as berries and currants, apples, cherries or pears.

Warm or chilled, all the fruit soups in this chapter are delicious either way. Serve hot straight from the soup maker, or leave to cool for a while and then chill to serve cold.

Apricot, Apple and Cardamom Soup

A warming and comforting soup. Cardamom adds a spicy-sweet flavour. Use other dried ready-to-eat fruits such as cranberries or pears.

Serves 4–6

2 dessert apples
9 ready-to-eat dried apricots
300 ml/ ½ pint unsweetened apple juice
450 ml/16 fl oz water
2 tbsp clear honey
¼ tsp ground cardamom

Thick natural yogurt, to serve

1. Peel, core and finely chop the apples. Cut each apricot in half and cut into thin slices.
2. *Blender-style soup maker* – Place everything in the glass jar and cover with the lid. Set the timer to 20 minutes and the temperature to high. Stir to mix. Bring to the boil, reduce the heat to simmer and cook for the remaining time using the stir button occasionally. Blend to the consistency you prefer.
3. If necessary, sweeten to taste with extra honey. Ladle or pour the hot soup into bowls. Top each bowl with a spoonful of yogurt and serve immediately.

Jug-style soup maker
Put all the prepared ingredients (step 1 above) and other ingredients into the metal jug. (The level of total ingredients must be above the minimum mark and below the maximum. If necessary, top up with unsweetened fruit juice or water.) Secure the lid in place. Select the purée function and leave to cook. If necessary, sweeten to taste with extra honey and serve as in step 3 above.

Nutty Peach and Almond Soup

A lovely delicate perfumed soup. Would be good made with nectarines as well.

Serves 4–6

5 ripe peaches
60 g/2 ¼ oz soft brown sugar
60 g/2 ¼ oz ground almonds
1 tsp lemon juice
300 ml/ ½ pint white grape juice
450 ml/16 fl oz water

Toasted almonds, to serve

1. Halve the peaches and remove the stones. Cut into small pieces.
2. *Blender-style soup maker* – Place everything in the glass jar and cover with the lid. Set the timer to 20 minutes and the temperature to high. Stir to mix. Bring to the boil, reduce the heat to simmer and cook for the remaining time using the stir button occasionally. Blend to the consistency you prefer.
3. If necessary, sweeten to taste with extra sugar. Ladle or pour the hot soup into bowls and scatter over a few toasted almonds. Serve immediately.

Jug-style soup maker
Put the prepared peaches (step 1 above) and other ingredients into the metal jug. (The level of total ingredients must be above the minimum mark and below the maximum. If necessary, top up with unsweetened fruit juice or water.) Secure the lid in place. Select the purée function and leave to cook. If necessary, sweeten to taste with extra sugar and serve as in step 3 above.

Chilled Cherry and Almond Soup

This soup freezes well and can be served hot or cold.

Serves 4–6

650 g/1 lb 7 oz pitted cherries, fresh or frozen
300 ml/ ½ pint unsweetened orange juice
300 ml/ ½ pint red wine
150 ml/ ¼ pint water
3 tbsp caster sugar
3 tbsp lemon juice
¼ tsp ground cardamom
2 tbsp ground almonds
1 tbsp Kirsch (optional)
Small handful of toasted chopped almonds

Soured cream and crushed amaretti biscuits, to serve

1. Cut each of the cherries in half.
2. *Blender-style soup maker* – Place everything except the toasted chopped almonds and kirsch into the glass jar and cover with the lid. Set the timer to 20 minutes and the temperature to high. Stir to mix. Bring to the boil, reduce the heat to simmer and cook for the remaining time using the stir button occasionally. Blend to the consistency you prefer. Remove the measuring cup and, if using, pour in the kirsch. Replace the cup and blend a second or two.
3. Ladle or pour the soup into a large bowl, leave to cool and chill until required. Stir the toasted chopped almonds into the soup. To serve ladle into bowls and top each with a spoonful of soured cream and a sprinkling of crushed biscuit.

Jug-style soup maker
Thaw the cherries, if frozen.

Put the prepared cherries (step 1 above) and other ingredients, except the toasted chopped almonds and kirsch, into the metal jug. (The level of total ingredients must be above the minimum mark and below the maximum. If necessary, top up with unsweetened fruit juice or water.) Secure the lid in place. Select the purée function and leave to cook. (If using the kirsch, remove the lid, pour in and blend for a second or two.) Serve as in step 3 above.

Blueberry and Apple Soup

Frozen blueberries can be used in the blender-style soup maker, but thaw blueberries to use them in the jug-style machine.

Serves 4–6

4 dessert apples
350 g/12 oz blueberries, fresh or frozen
300 ml/½ pint white wine or white grape juice
450 ml/16 fl oz water
3 tbsp caster sugar
¼ tsp ground cloves
¼ tsp ground cinnamon

Double cream or natural yogurt, to serve

1. Peel, core and finely chop the apples.
2. *Blender-style soup maker* – Place everything in the glass jar and cover with the lid. Set the timer to 20 minutes and the temperature to high. Stir to mix. Bring to the boil, reduce the heat to simmer and cook for the remaining time using the stir button occasionally. Blend to the consistency you prefer.
3. Ladle or pour the hot soup into bowls. Top each bowl with a spoonful of double cream or natural yogurt and serve immediately.

Jug-style soup maker
Thaw the blueberries, if frozen.

Put the prepared apples (step 1 above) and other ingredients, into the metal jug. (The level of total ingredients must be above the minimum mark and below the maximum. If necessary, top up with unsweetened fruit juice or water.) Secure the lid in place. Select the chunky function and leave to cook. Use the blend button if necessary. Serve as in step 3 above.

Grape and Elderflower Soup

Choose either green or black grapes, and go for those packed with lots of flavour.

Serves 4–6

1 orange
Large bunch of small seedless grapes, about 650 g/1 lb 7 oz
300 ml/½ pint white or red grape juice, depending on the grape colour
425 ml/¾ pint water
3 tbsp clear honey or caster sugar
5 tbsp elderflower syrup
¼ tsp ground cinnamon

Toasted brioche bread, to serve

1. Grate the rind from the orange, cut in half and squeeze out the juice. Pull the grapes from the stalks and cut each in half.
2. *Blender-style soup maker* – Place everything in the glass jar and cover with the lid. Set the timer to 25 minutes and the temperature to high. Stir to mix. Bring to the boil, reduce the heat to simmer and cook for the remaining time using the stir button occasionally. Blend to the consistency you prefer.
3. Ladle or pour the hot soup into bowls. Serve immediately with slices of toasted brioche.

Jug-style soup maker
Put all the prepared ingredients (step 1 above) and other ingredients into the metal jug. (The level of total ingredients must be above the minimum mark and below the maximum. If necessary, top up with unsweetened fruit juice or water.) Secure the lid in place. Select the chunky function and leave to cook. Use the blend button if necessary. Serve as in step 3 above.

Melon and Ginger Soup

There are many types of melons available, often sold in wedges. Try two different types together.

Serves 4–6

1 melon, to give about 700 g/1 lb 9 oz flesh
5 cm/2 inch piece of fresh root ginger
4–6 small mint leaves
300 ml/½ pint unsweetened apple juice
300 ml/½ pint water
4 tbsp clear honey or soft brown sugar
2 tsp cornflour
150 ml/¼ pint crème fraîche

Crème fraîche and chopped crystallized ginger to serve

1. Peel the melon, cut in half and scoop out the seeds. Cut the flesh into small cubes, about 2.5 cm/1 inch. Coarsely grate the root ginger, gather together with your hand and squeeze the juice into a cup. Discard the pulp.
2. *Blender-style soup maker* – Place everything except the crème fraîche into the glass jar and cover with the lid. Set the timer to 15 minutes and the temperature to high. Stir to mix. Bring to the boil, reduce the heat to simmer and cook for the remaining time using the stir button occasionally. Add the crème fraîche, replace the lid and blend to the consistency you prefer.
3. Ladle or pour the hot soup into bowls. Serve immediately topped with a spoon of crème fraîche and a scattering of chopped crystallized ginger.

Jug-style soup maker
Put all the prepared ingredients (step 1 above) and other ingredients, except the crème fraîche, into the metal jug. (The level of total ingredients must be above the minimum mark and below the maximum. If necessary, top up with unsweetened fruit juice or water.) Secure the lid in place. Select the purée function and leave to cook. Remove the lid and add the crème fraîche. Replace the lid and use the blend button for 2–3 seconds. Serve as in step 3 above.

Orchard Fruit Soup

A soup that's quick to make, using a bag of prepared frozen fruits. If using fresh fruits, just halve, core and chop.

Serves 4–6

500 g/1 lb 2 oz frozen orchard fruits, such as berries, currants, pears, apples
300 ml/½ pint sweet cider or apple juice
300 ml/½ pint apple juice
150 ml/¼ pint water
2 tbsp caster sugar
2 tsp cornflour
½ tsp ground allspice

Tiny thin shortbread biscuits, to serve

1. Cut any large pieces of the fruit into small chunks.
2. *Blender-style soup maker* – Place everything in the glass jar and cover with the lid. Set the timer to 20 minutes and the temperature to high. Stir to mix. Bring just to the boil, reduce the heat to simmer and cook for the remaining time using the stir button occasionally. Blend to the consistency you prefer.
3. Ladle or pour the hot soup into bowls. Serve immediately with shortbread biscuits.

Jug-style soup maker
Thaw the fruit, if frozen.

Put all the prepared ingredients (step 1 above) and other ingredients into the metal jug. (The level of total ingredients must be above the minimum mark and below the maximum. If necessary, top up with unsweetened fruit juice or water.) Secure the lid in place. Select the chunky function and leave to cook. Use the blend button for a few seconds. Serve as in step 3 above.

Strawberry and Raspberry Soup

Perfect to make when there is a glut of fruit around. If serving cold, add a splash of sparkling wine, prosecco or champagne for a special occasion.

Serves 4–6

650 g/1 lb 7 oz ripe strawberries
1 vanilla pod or ½ tsp vanilla extract
250 g/9 oz raspberries
300 ml/½ pint unsweetened orange juice
400 ml/14 fl oz water
4 tbsp caster sugar
2 tbsp lemon juice

Single cream and grated white chocolate, to serve

1. Remove any green stalks from the strawberries and halve or quarter, if large. Split the vanilla pod and scrape out the seeds to use in the soup. (Don't discard the pod – put it into a jar of sugar. The sugar absorbs the flavour, so use when baking or making desserts.)
2. *Blender-style soup maker* – Place everything in the glass jar and cover with the lid. Set the timer to 15 minutes and the temperature to high. Stir to mix. Bring to the boil, reduce the heat to simmer and cook for the remaining time using the stir button occasionally. Blend to the consistency you prefer.
3. Ladle or pour the hot soup into bowls. Top each bowl with a swirl of cream and sprinkle over a little grated chocolate. Serve immediately.

Jug-style soup maker
Put all the prepared ingredients (step 1 above) and other ingredients into the metal jug. (The level of total ingredients must be above the minimum mark and below the maximum. If necessary, top up with unsweetened fruit juice or water.) Secure the lid in place. Select the chunky function and leave to cook. Use the blend button for a few seconds. Serve as in step 3 above.

8

IN THE BOWL AND
ON THE SIDE

A piping-hot bowl of soup can be enhanced still further by well-judged additions and accompaniments – savoury extras making for perfect combinations.

In the bowl – for swirling in or scattering over the soup – try yogurt or cream, with a host of herby or tangy flavourings stirred in, or add crispy, spicy croûtons, a splash of oil or a sprinkling of tasted seeds.

On the side – what better than hot buttered savoury scones to go with a large warming bowl of soup, or breadsticks rolled in mixed seeds and grated Parmesan?

A few simple additions like these can turn a serving of soup into a special occasion. So here are a couple of recipes, some hints and tips and lots of ideas to give your soups that extra zing.

Chive and Mustard Scones

Warm savoury scones are delicious served alongside a bowl of hot soup. Can be frozen and reheated. Serve with butter.

Makes 8–12

1 medium egg
50 g/1 ¼ oz butter
225 g/8 oz self-raising flour, plus extra for rolling
1 tsp baking powder
2 tbsp freshly chopped chives
2 tsp wholegrain mustard
About 5 tbsp milk, plus extra for brushing

1. Preheat the oven to 220°C, Fan 205°C, Gas 7.
2. Lightly beat the egg in a small cup and cut the butter into small cubes.
3. Sift the flour and baking powder into a large bowl and add the butter. Using your fingertips, rub the butter into the flour until the mixture resembles fine crumbs. Stir in the chopped chives.
4. With a round-bladed table knife, mix the wholegrain mustard, beaten egg and sufficient milk into the mixture to make a soft dough.
5. Turn onto a lightly floured surface and knead gently until smooth. Roll or pat the dough into a rough round, about 1 cm/½ inch thick. Cut into discs, squares or shapes using cutters or a sharp knife.
6. Arrange the scones on a baking sheet and brush the tops with a little milk. Put into the hot oven and cook for 10–12 minutes until well risen, golden brown and cooked through. Cool on a wire rack.

Seeded Parmesan Breadsticks

Make a batch of breadsticks and freeze the excess. In place of the seeds, try chopped nuts.

Makes about 18–20, depending on size

1 white or brown bread mix
Flour, for kneading
2–3 tbsp grated Parmesan cheese
A selection of seeds, such as sesame, poppy, pumpkin or sunflower seeds
2–3 tbsp olive oil

1. Make up the bread dough mix following the packet instructions. Put into a bowl and cover with a clean cloth or oiled cling film. Leave in a warm place until doubled in size, about 35 minutes.
2. Turn the dough onto a floured surface and roughly roll or shape into a square. With a sharp knife cut into strips, the size doesn't matter. With floured hands, pull and roll each piece of dough into thin sticks.
3. Mix the Parmesan cheese and seeds on a tray and spread out. Brush the breadsticks with a little oil and roll in the seeds aiming for some to stick. Lift them onto greased baking trays and leave to rise for 15 minutes.
4. Preheat the oven to 200°C, Fan 185°C, Gas 6.
5. Put into the hot oven and bake for 12–15 minutes, depending on the size, until golden brown. Cool on a wire rack.

Things to Scatter, Sprinkle and Float
Just a small sprinkling or scattering of savoury extras over a bowl of soup can liven up a simple soup by adding complementary flavour and crunch. Or try a toasty cheese float, perfect on tomato or onion soup.

Crunchy Spiced Croûtons
Tear sourdough bread into rough, bite-sized pieces. Heat some sunflower oil in a non-stick frying pan together with a sliced red chilli, a crushed clove of garlic and a few coriander seeds. When the oil is hot, stir in the pieces of bread and cook quickly until crisp and golden. Drain on kitchen paper. Discard the chilli, garlic and seeds.

Toasty Cheese Floats
Cut thick slices from a French stick or baguette and toast on both sides under a hot grill. Spread one side with garlic butter and top with grated hard cheese or slices of goats' cheese. Pop back under the hot grill until golden and bubbling.

Toasted Seeds and Nuts

Keep a screw-topped jar of toasted seeds or nuts handy in a kitchen cupboard. I like to scatter a tiny sprinkling on a blob of yogurt floating on the soup. I like pine nuts, blanched almonds and sunflower seeds. Heat a non-stick pan and dry-fry the nuts and seeds until toasty. Don't leave them, they will cook very quickly. Immediately tip them onto a plate and leave to cool. Then spoon into a storage jar.

Bacon Bits

Cut the rind off rashers of back or smoked bacon. Put the bacon under a hot grill and cook on both sides until crispy. With scissors, cut into small pieces and immediately scatter over hot soup.

Things to Drizzle, Spoon and Swirl

Mix and match, choose your favourite combination.

Pour 300 ml/½ pint single or double cream, or natural yogurt, or crème fraîche, or fromage frais, or even mayonnaise, into a bowl. Stir in the flavourings of your choice and a little seasoning, adding more milk if necessary depending on whether you are going to drizzle, spoon or swirl the mix into a bowl of soup.

Here are some suggestions:

- 1 tbsp ready-made wholegrain mustard and a small handful of finely chopped parsley.
- Small handful of chopped fennel leaves and a few toasted pine nuts, chopped, if large.
- 3 skinned and finely chopped tomatoes and a few chopped chives.
- Small handful of torn basil leaves and a few chopped or broken walnuts.
- 1 finely chopped red pimiento and a few oregano leaves.
- 2 tbsp tomato ketchup.

Drizzle a few tiny drops of oil onto the surface of the soup just before serving. Use plain olive oil or one of the flavoured oils, such as walnut, sesame or hazelnut or those flavoured with herbs, but use them very sparingly.

INDEX